LINUX
— for —
BEGINNERS

A Practical and Comprehensive Guide to Learn Linux Operating System and Master Linux Command Line. Contains Self-Evaluation Tests to Verify Your Learning Level.

ETHEM MINING

Copyright © 2026

All rights reserved

No part of this publication may be reproduced, duplicated, or transmitted in any form or by any means, electronic, mechanical, scanning, photocopying, recording, or otherwise, without prior written permission from the publisher.

The information provided herein is believed to be accurate; however, any liability arising from the use or misuse of any policies, processes, or directions contained within is solely the responsibility of the recipient. Under no circumstances shall the publisher be held liable for any damages or monetary loss resulting from the information presented, whether directly or indirectly.

Legal Notice

This book is copyright protected and is intended for personal use only. You cannot amend, distribute, sell, quote, use, or paraphrase any part of the content without the consent of the author or copyright owner. Legal action will be pursued if this is breached.

ABOUT THE AUTHOR

My name is Ethem Mining, and I was born in Baltimore in November 1973, the same year the first computer was installed in the White House. Coincidence or not, technology has fascinated me ever since. It's always drawn me in, almost like a magnet.

I wrote my first computer program at the age of thirteen. It was a simple application written in Pascal, but it was mine, and it gave me a way to turn imagination into something real. From that moment on, technology became more than an interest; it became a passion.

As my studies progressed, I found myself increasingly drawn to the world of cybersecurity. It's a field that is constantly evolving and endlessly challenging. In cybersecurity, standing still means falling behind. You must always stay one step ahead of those with malicious intent, who are just as skilled, motivated, and passionate about information technology. That challenge is what makes the field so compelling and keeps continuous learning essential.

For many years, I wanted to share this passion with others. That motivation led me to write a series of books aimed primarily at beginners, designed to introduce readers to the fundamentals of Linux, programming, and cybersecurity in a clear and approachable way.

I welcome your suggestions, requests, and most importantly, your criticisms. Every message I receive is an opportunity to improve, and I value each one. You can reach me at **contact@ethemmining.com**

Thank you, and happy reading!

Table of Contents

Introduction vii

Chapter 1: What is Linux? 1
    Chapter 1 Quiz 12

Chapter 2: Choosing Your Distribution 15
    Chapter 2 Quiz 36

Chapter 3: Installing Linux 39
    Chapter 3 Quiz 56

Chapter 4: The Linux Shell 59
    Chapter 4 Quiz 80

Chapter 5: Essential Linux Commands 83
    Chapter 5 Quiz 108

Chapter 6: Package Management 111
    Chapter 6 Quiz 122

Chapter 7: Users and Privileges 125
    Chapter 7 Quiz 140

Chapter 8: Networking 143
    Chapter 8 Quiz 160

Chapter 9: Troubleshooting Linux 163
    Chapter 9 Quiz 178

Chapter 10: Alternatives to Windows Applications 181
    Chapter 10 Quiz 194

Conclusion 197

APPENDIX 199

GLOSSARY 212

INTRODUCTION

Linux is a powerful and flexible operating system used on personal computers, servers, development systems, and cloud infrastructure around the world. Unlike proprietary systems, Linux allows you to shape your environment to suit your needs. It places a strong emphasis on stability, security, privacy, and access to a vast ecosystem of free and open source software. With the right approach, it can also extend the useful life of older hardware that may struggle with more resource intensive operating systems.

This book is designed as a practical guide for beginners and focuses on Debian-based distributions such as Debian and Linux Mint. Rather than relying on desktop screenshots, the emphasis is on understanding how Linux works beneath the surface. This approach helps you develop skills that transfer across many Linux systems, regardless of the desktop environment you choose.

Throughout this book, you will explore essential topics including what Linux is, how to choose the right distribution, installing Linux, understanding the Linux file system, working with the shell, and managing software packages. Each chapter builds on the previous one to help you develop a clear and practical foundation.

Step-by-step explanations and realistic command examples guide you through each topic. By the end of this book, you will have a working understanding of Linux and the confidence to use it independently, along with a strong foundation for further learning if you choose to continue exploring the platform.

How to Use This Book

This guide is designed to be read from beginning to end, as each chapter builds on concepts introduced earlier. If you are new to Linux, following the chapters in order will provide the clearest path to understanding.

The focus is on understanding how Linux operates beneath the surface, with particular attention to the command line. Even if you primarily use a graphical interface, becoming familiar with the shell will make you more capable and confident when working with a Linux system.

Explanations are paired with practical examples to help you understand not only how commands work, but also why they behave the way they do. You are encouraged to experiment in a safe environment, such as a virtual machine, where mistakes can be made without affecting your primary system.

Each chapter concludes with a summary and a short quiz to reinforce key ideas.

The Appendix provides quick reference material for commonly used commands and core Linux concepts. The Glossary explains important technical terms.

How to Read Command Examples:

Commands in this book are shown in a simplified format to make them easier to understand. Some examples use placeholder words such as *filename*, *directory_name*, *path*, *source*, or *destination*. These placeholders represent values that you replace with the actual name of a file or directory on your system.

For example:

```
rm filename
```

In practice, you would replace *filename* with the name of a real file.

"Intelligence is the ability to avoid doing work, yet getting the work done."

— Linus Torvalds

CHAPTER 1
What is Linux?

So you have decided to use Linux, or at least learn more about it. You are in the right place! Linux refers to a family of operating systems built around the Linux kernel. Like Windows and macOS, these systems manage computer hardware and provide a platform on which applications can run.

This chapter introduces Linux at a high level and helps you understand what it is, why it exists, and how to think about it before you begin using it. Rather than diving into commands or configuration, the focus here is on core concepts that will make the rest of the book easier to follow and help you build confidence as you move forward.

What is an Operating System?

An operating system, commonly abbreviated as OS, is the software that manages a computer's hardware and software resources. It controls how hardware components such as the processor, memory, and storage devices are used, while also providing a platform on which applications can run.

Most importantly, the operating system allows you to interact with the computer without needing to understand complex machine instructions.

In simple terms, the operating system acts as an intermediary between the user, the applications you run, and the computer's hardware. When you open a program, save a file, or connect a device, the operating system manages these interactions behind the scenes.

The diagram below illustrates this relationship:

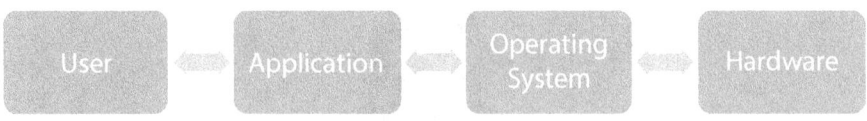

This relationship is fundamental and applies to all modern operating systems, including Windows, macOS, and Linux.

What Makes Linux Different?

What makes Linux unique compared to many other operating systems is not how it looks on the surface, but how it is designed and developed. At its core, Linux emphasizes transparency, flexibility, and user control.

Unlike proprietary operating systems, Linux is open source. This means the source code is publicly available and can be examined, modified, and improved by anyone. As a result, development happens collaboratively, and users are not locked into a single vendor's decisions or business model.

Many of these ideas are influenced by the Unix operating system, which shaped how Linux systems are structured and used. Unix introduced design principles such as modular design, user control, and the concept that many parts of the system are treated as files.

Building on these ideas, Linux systems are designed to be highly flexible. Users can choose which components are installed, how the system behaves, and how software is installed and updated, typically through centralized package management. This flexibility allows Linux to run on everything from lightweight systems on older hardware to large servers and cloud infrastructure.

The Linux Philosophy

These Unix-inspired design ideas shape how many Linux tools and utilities are built.

One important principle is that programs should perform a single task well. Instead of creating large applications that attempt to do everything, Linux encourages the use of smaller tools that focus on one specific function.

Another key idea is that programs should work well together. The output of one program can often be used as the input for another, allowing users to combine simple tools to perform more complex tasks.

These tools often operate on simple text streams, which makes it easy to connect programs and process data in flexible ways. This approach is commonly used from the command line, where small tools can be combined to build powerful workflows.

This philosophy is often summarized as: *"Do one thing and do it well."*

Where Linux Is Used Today

Linux is widely used across many areas of modern computing, often in ways that are not immediately visible to everyday users. While desktop Linux systems exist, the platform is especially dominant in server, cloud, and large-scale infrastructure environments.

Most websites and online services run on Linux-based servers. Large technology companies, financial institutions, research organizations, and government agencies rely on Linux for its stability, security, and ability to operate continuously for long periods with minimal interruption. If you use online banking, streaming services, or social media platforms, there is a strong likelihood that Linux systems are involved behind the scenes.

Linux also forms the foundation of many cloud computing platforms. Virtual machines, containers, and distributed systems are frequently built on Linux because it can be customized for efficiency and reliability.

Mobile devices represent another major area of Linux usage. The Android operating system, which powers the majority of smartphones worldwide, is built on a modified Linux kernel. Although the user experience differs from a traditional Linux desktop, the underlying technology shares common principles.

A Brief History of Linux

Linux began in 1991 when **Linus Torvalds**, then a computer science student, started developing a free operating system kernel as a personal project. He released the code publicly and invited others to contribute.

This collaborative approach quickly attracted developers from around the world. Over time, the Linux kernel was combined with tools and utilities from the open source community to form complete operating systems that could be used by anyone.

This open development model laid the foundation for the Linux ecosystem that continues to evolve today.

High-Level Structure of a Linux System

At a high level, a Linux system can be thought of as having two main parts: the **kernel** and **user space**. Although Linux is often referred to as an operating system, the term technically refers to the Linux kernel, the core component that manages system resources, including hardware.

A complete Linux operating system is formed when the kernel is combined with user space programs, libraries, and utilities. In practice, these components are assembled and distributed as Linux distributions.

The **kernel** manages system resources such as the CPU, memory, storage devices, and input and output hardware. Applications do not interact directly with hardware. Instead, they communicate with the kernel, which coordinates access to these resources.

User space contains everything outside the kernel. This includes applications, system utilities, background services, and user interfaces. Programs running in user space rely on the kernel whenever they need access to hardware or other system resources.

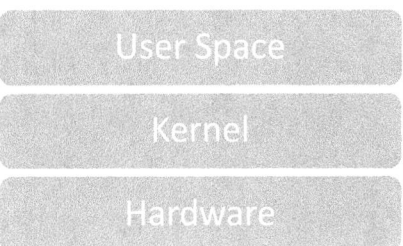

This separation between user space and kernel improves stability and security by preventing applications from directly controlling hardware or interfering with critical system functions.

Files and Processes in Linux (Conceptual Overview)

Linux organizes information using a hierarchical file system. Files and directories are arranged in a structured tree that begins at a single top-level location known as the **root directory** (/). From this starting point, every file and directory on the system can be located through a series of nested directories.

In Linux and other Unix-like systems, many parts of the operating system are treated as files. Devices, system information, and configuration data can appear in the file system and be accessed using the same tools used for ordinary files.

Programs running on a Linux system are known as **processes**. Each process represents an active instance of a program currently being executed by the system. Linux can run many processes at the same time while keeping them isolated from one another, meaning a failure or crash in one program normally does not affect other running programs. The kernel controls how processes access system resources, helping maintain overall system stability.

Detailed exploration of the file system and process management will be introduced later once you are comfortable working with the command line.

System Tools and the GNU Project

While the Linux kernel forms the core of the system, a complete Linux environment also includes many essential tools and utilities that allow users to interact with the system.

Many of these tools originate from the **GNU Project**, an open source initiative started in the 1980s with the goal of creating a free Unix-like operating system. The GNU project developed many of the foundational programs commonly used on Linux systems today.

For example, many familiar command-line utilities such as ls, cp, mv, cat, and pwd are part of the GNU Core Utilities, a collection of basic programs used to perform everyday tasks on the system.

When the Linux kernel is combined with these tools and utilities, it forms a usable operating system environment. Because many of these tools originate from the GNU Project, some people refer to Linux systems more precisely as **GNU/Linux**, acknowledging the contributions of both the Linux kernel and GNU software.

Graphical Desktop Environments

Linux systems can include graphical desktop environments similar to those found in Windows and macOS. These environments provide windows, menus, icons, and mouse interaction, allowing users to work with the system visually.

Many different desktop environments exist, and their appearance and behavior can vary significantly between Linux distributions. Because of this variation, this book focuses primarily on foundational concepts and command-line skills that apply across Linux systems.

This approach ensures that the knowledge gained in this book remains useful regardless of the specific desktop environment in use.

What Comes Next?

Linux is not a single packaged product created by one company. It is a collection of components assembled in different ways by various communities and organizations. These assembled versions are called distributions.

Understanding this structure is essential before installation, because choosing a distribution determines the tools, package management system, and default environment you will work with.

Chapter 1 Summary

- Linux refers to a family of operating systems built around the Linux kernel.

- Linux is open source, flexible, and developed collaboratively by a global community.

- A Linux system is structured around two main parts: the kernel and user space.

- Programs run as processes, and data is organized within a hierarchical file system.

- Many common system tools originate from the GNU Project, forming the foundation of the Linux command-line environment.

In the next chapter, you will learn how Linux distributions are organized and how to choose a distribution that fits your needs.

CHAPTER 1 QUIZ

Try these questions to check your understanding of the key concepts from this chapter. The answer key is provided on the next page.

1. **What is the primary role of an operating system?**
    A) To manufacture computer hardware
    B) To manage hardware resources and allow applications to run
    C) To replace all installed software
    D) To connect computers to the internet only

2. **Linux is an operating system built around the Linux kernel.**
    True or False

3. **Which statement best describes open source software?**
    A) It can only be used by developers
    B) Its source code is publicly available to examine and modify
    C) It cannot be changed once released
    D) It requires payment to use legally

4. **Which part of a Linux system directly manages hardware resources such as CPU and memory?**

A) User space
B) Desktop environment
C) Kernel
D) Application layer

5. **In Linux, programs that are currently running are called processes.**

    True or False

6. **Why does this book focus on command-line skills rather than a specific graphical desktop environment?**
    A) Because Linux cannot run graphical interfaces
    B) Because command-line skills work across different distributions and environments
    C) Because desktop environments are identical on all systems
    D) Because graphical tools are no longer used in Linux

CHAPTER 1 ANSWER KEY

1. **B** — The operating system manages hardware and provides a platform for applications to run

2. **True** — Linux is defined as an operating system built around the Linux kernel

3. **B** — Open source software allows anyone to view, modify, and improve the code

4. **C** — The kernel is the core component that manages hardware and system resources

5. **True** — A process represents a running instance of a program

6. **B** — Command-line skills remain useful across different distributions despite graphical differences

CHAPTER 2
Choosing Your Distribution

Choosing a Linux distribution is often one of the first challenges beginners face. Unlike Windows or macOS, Linux is not a single product but a family of operating systems known as distributions. Each distribution combines the Linux kernel with different software, tools, and default settings.

At first, the number of available distributions can feel overwhelming. This variety exists because Linux is designed to be flexible and adaptable to many different use cases. While distributions may look different or make different choices by default, they all share the same core principles and underlying technology.

If you are new to Linux, it is important to understand that there is no single "best" distribution. Most Linux systems behave similarly beneath the surface, and skills learned on one distribution transfer easily to others. Your first choice is simply a starting point, not a permanent decision.

This chapter introduces several popular Linux distributions and explains their strengths, intended audiences, and typical use cases. The goal is not to cover every available option, but to help you make an informed and confident choice before moving on to installation in the next chapter.

What is a Linux Distribution?

A Linux distribution, often shortened to *distro*, is a complete operating system built around the Linux kernel. While the kernel is the core component that manages hardware and system resources, a distribution includes everything else needed to make the system usable.

This typically includes system utilities, software management tools, default applications, installation programs, and one or more user interfaces. A distribution defines how Linux is packaged, installed, updated, and presented to the user.

Different distributions make different design choices, such as which software is included by default, how updates are delivered, and how system configuration is handled.

Why Multiple Distributions Exist

Linux is developed in an open and collaborative way rather than being controlled by a single organization. Because the Linux kernel and much of the surrounding software are open source, individuals and groups are free to assemble systems that serve different goals.

Some distributions prioritize long-term stability, others focus on ease of use, performance, security, or access to newer software. These differences reflect design priorities rather than incompatibilities between systems.

At this point, it helps to step back and consider what typically influences these choices. The following graphic highlights some of the common questions developers and users ask when selecting or designing a Linux distribution.

Where are you installing Linux?	How much experience do you have?	What kind of software support do you want?
What do you want your desktop experience to be?	How customizable do you want the OS to be?	How often do you want support updates?

Taken together, these factors explain why no single Linux distribution fits every situation. Linux is designed to be adaptable, allowing systems to be tailored for personal computers, servers, development environments, or specialized use cases without forcing a single standard configuration.

The following sections introduce several popular Linux distributions and describe their typical use cases and target audiences.

Ubuntu

Ubuntu is one of the most widely known Linux distributions and is developed by Canonical. It is based on Debian and follows a regular release cycle, with long-term support (LTS) versions released every two years.

Ubuntu was created with the goal of making Linux more accessible to a broader audience. This focus on usability, predictable releases, and broad hardware support has helped Ubuntu become a common entry point into the Linux ecosystem.

Ubuntu balances stability with modern features. It includes a polished installation process, sensible defaults, and a large collection of preconfigured software, making it widely used on personal computers, servers, and cloud platforms.

Although Ubuntu introduces its own tools and design choices, it retains the same underlying Linux architecture as Debian. Skills learned on Ubuntu transfer directly to other Debian-based systems.

Difficulty rating: Good for beginners.

Long-term support: Interim releases every 6 months, with long-term support (LTS) releases available every 2 years.

Pros

- Regular updates on a fixed release cycle with defined support periods.
- Long-term support (LTS) releases provide 5 years of security updates.
- Beginner-friendly with sensible defaults.
- Widely used, with extensive documentation and community support available online.

Cons

- Regular updates can introduce noticeable changes, particularly in non-LTS releases.
- Non-LTS releases receive only 9 months of security updates.
- The default GNOME desktop can be more resource intensive on older hardware.

Linux Mint

Linux Mint is a popular Linux distribution designed with ease of use and familiarity in mind. It is based on Ubuntu and Debian, providing a stable foundation, long-term support options, and access to a large software ecosystem.

Its primary goal is to offer a comfortable experience for users who are new to Linux, especially those transitioning from Windows. The desktop environments follow a traditional layout, making everyday tasks such as navigating menus, managing files, and adjusting settings feel intuitive.

Linux Mint includes many commonly used applications by default, reducing the amount of setup required after installation. It also avoids frequent interface changes, helping maintain a consistent and predictable experience.

Beneath the surface, Linux Mint behaves like other Debian-based systems. The same file system structure, package management tools, and command-line concepts apply, allowing skills learned here to transfer easily to other Linux distributions.

For users seeking a stable and beginner-friendly starting point, Linux Mint is often an excellent first choice.

Difficulty rating: Excellent for beginners.

Long-term support: Based on Ubuntu LTS releases, with approximately 5 years of security updates.

Pros

- Very beginner-friendly, especially for users coming from Windows.
- Clean and familiar desktop layouts (Cinnamon, MATE, and Xfce).
- Based on Ubuntu LTS, providing long-term stability and security updates.
- Strong community support and clear documentation.

Cons

- Slower adoption of newer software compared to non-LTS distributions.
- Smaller commercial backing compared to Ubuntu.
- Fewer official desktop options than some other distributions.

Debian GNU/Linux

Debian GNU/Linux is one of the oldest and most influential Linux distributions. It is developed by a large, independent community and follows a strong commitment to free and open source software.

The Debian project was created to provide a fully community-driven operating system, developed transparently and without commercial control. This principle-first approach has shaped Debian's careful software selection and long-term reliability.

Debian is best known for its stability. Software in Debian's stable releases is extensively tested, resulting in a system that changes slowly and predictably.

While Debian can be used as a desktop operating system, it typically requires more user involvement during installation and configuration than beginner-focused distributions.

Difficulty rating: Intermediate.

Long-term support: Stable releases receive approximately 5 years of security updates through the Debian Security and LTS projects.

Pros

- Extremely stable and reliable.
- Strong commitment to free and open source software.
- Large software repositories with well-tested packages.
- Excellent documentation and community resources.
- Forms the foundation for many other Linux distributions.

Cons

- Slower access to newer software versions.
- More manual setup compared to beginner-focused distributions.
- Less polished desktop experience by default.

Fedora

Fedora is a Linux distribution sponsored by Red Hat and developed by a large open source community. It is commonly used as a platform for introducing newer Linux technologies as they become available.

Fedora was created to move Linux forward by adopting modern software and standards early. It often serves as a proving ground for technologies that later appear in enterprise and long-term support distributions.

Fedora focuses on providing up-to-date software while maintaining a clean, well-structured system. The default Fedora Workstation edition uses the GNOME desktop and stays close to upstream design, avoiding heavy customization.

Fedora is frequently chosen by developers and technically inclined users who want early access to new features while working within a disciplined and well-maintained system.

Difficulty rating: Intermediate.

Long-term support: Fixed release cycle with approximately 13 months of support per release.

Pros

- Provides access to newer software and Linux technologies.
- Closely aligned with upstream open source projects.
- Strong backing from Red Hat and an active community.
- Well suited for development and learning modern Linux systems.
- Clean and consistent system design.

Cons

- Shorter support lifecycle compared to LTS-based distributions.
- More frequent upgrades required to stay supported.
- Default GNOME desktop can be demanding on older hardware.
- Less focused on beginner convenience than Ubuntu or Linux Mint.

openSUSE

openSUSE is a long-standing Linux distribution known for its structured approach to system management and configuration. It is closely associated with SUSE Linux Enterprise and reflects many enterprise-oriented design principles.

The openSUSE project began as a community counterpart to SUSE's commercial Linux offerings, with the goal of making enterprise-grade technologies more broadly accessible. This relationship has strongly influenced its emphasis on reliability and control.

openSUSE is available in two main editions. **Leap** focuses on stability and predictability, while **Tumbleweed** provides a rolling-release model with continuously updated software.

One of openSUSE's defining features is **YaST** (Yet another Setup Tool), which offers a centralized interface for configuring software, users, networking, and system services.

Difficulty rating: Intermediate.

Long-term support: Leap offers a stable release model with long support periods. Tumbleweed is rolling release and remains supported through continuous updates.

Pros

- Excellent system administration tools, especially YaST.
- Two clear options: stable (Leap) or rolling (Tumbleweed).
- Reliable and well-organized system design.
- Strong documentation and a mature community.
- Suitable for both desktops and servers.

Cons

- Less common for beginners, so fewer beginner-focused tutorials than Ubuntu-based systems.
- Choosing between Leap and Tumbleweed can be confusing at first.
- Rolling-release updates in Tumbleweed require more attention than fixed-release systems.

Arch Linux

Arch Linux is a lightweight, rolling-release Linux distribution designed around simplicity, transparency, and user control. Rather than providing a preconfigured system, Arch gives users a minimal base and expects them to build the system according to their needs.

Arch follows a rolling-release model, meaning software is continuously updated instead of being released in fixed versions. This allows users to access very recent software, but it also requires regular maintenance and attention to system changes.

A key principle of Arch Linux is that the user should understand how the system is assembled and configured. Installation and setup are largely manual, encouraging users to learn how Linux components fit together rather than relying on automated tools.

Arch Linux is commonly used by experienced users who want full control over their system and are comfortable troubleshooting issues as they arise. It is often chosen as a learning platform for gaining a deeper understanding of Linux internals.

Difficulty rating: Advanced.

Long-term support: Rolling release with continuous updates; no fixed support period.

Pros

- Access to very recent software and kernel versions.
- Excellent documentation, particularly the Arch Wiki.
- High level of control over system configuration.
- Rolling-release model eliminates major version upgrades.

Cons

- Manual installation and setup require prior Linux knowledge.
- Rolling updates can occasionally introduce breaking changes.
- Not designed for beginners or users seeking a hands-off experience.
- Requires regular maintenance and user involvement.

Pop!_OS

Pop!_OS is a Linux distribution developed by System76, a company that builds and sells Linux-focused computers. It is based on Ubuntu and is designed to provide a streamlined, productivity-oriented desktop experience.

Pop!_OS was created to improve the Linux desktop for developers, creators, and technical users, with a strong focus on workflow and hardware compatibility. This background has influenced its emphasis on performance, keyboard-driven navigation, and integrated graphics support.

The distribution includes a customized desktop environment built on GNOME, with features such as automatic window tiling and simplified system configuration. These additions aim to reduce friction for users who spend long periods working on their systems.

Because Pop!_OS is based on Ubuntu, it benefits from long-term support releases, broad hardware compatibility, and access to Ubuntu's software repositories. At the same time, it introduces its own design choices that may feel different from more traditional desktop layouts.

Difficulty rating: Intermediate.

Long-term support: Based on Ubuntu LTS releases, with approximately 5 years of security updates.

Pros

- Optimized for productivity with built-in window tiling features.
- Strong hardware support, particularly for graphics cards and laptops.
- Based on Ubuntu LTS, providing stability and long-term security updates.
- Good documentation and support from System76.

Cons

- Desktop layout differs from traditional Windows-style environments.
- Less configurable out of the box than some other distributions.
- Smaller community compared to Ubuntu or Linux Mint.
- Some features are closely tied to the GNOME-based workflow.

Choosing the Right Distribution for You

After reviewing the different Linux distributions, the next step is deciding where to begin. While the number of options may seem large, most beginners only need to consider a few practical factors.

The most important consideration is **how you plan to use Linux**. For general desktop use, learning, and everyday tasks, a stable distribution with strong community support is usually the best starting point. If your goal is to explore Linux fundamentals without unnecessary complexity, choosing a widely used and well-documented distribution will make the learning process smoother.

Another factor is **how much system management you want to take on early**. Some distributions are designed to minimize setup and configuration, while others expect users to be more hands-on. Neither approach is better, but beginners often benefit from starting with a system that works well out of the box and allows deeper exploration over time.

For most new users, the following categories provide a helpful guide:

- **Beginner-friendly starting points:** Distributions such as Linux Mint and Ubuntu prioritize ease of use, stability, and documentation. They allow beginners to focus on learning Linux concepts without being overwhelmed by setup decisions.

- **Balanced and performance-focused options:** Distributions like MX Linux and Pop!_OS offer more control or performance while remaining accessible. These are good choices for users who want a bit more involvement without jumping into advanced territory.

- **Advanced learning platforms:** Distributions such as Arch Linux and Gentoo are best suited for users who intentionally want a hands-on learning experience and are comfortable troubleshooting and managing system complexity.

It's important to remember that your first distribution is not a permanent choice. Skills learned on one Linux system transfer easily to others, and switching distributions later is a normal part of learning.

The best approach is to start with a distribution that matches your comfort level today, gain experience, and explore other options as your confidence grows.

CHAPTER 2 QUIZ

Try these questions to check your understanding of the key concepts from this chapter. The answer key is provided on the next page.

1. **What is a Linux distribution (distro)?**
    A) A hardware device designed to run Linux
    B) A complete operating system built around the Linux kernel
    C) A graphical theme for Linux desktops
    D) A programming language used on Linux systems

2. **Linux distributions can differ in appearance, included software, and target users while sharing the same underlying kernel.**
    True or False

3. **Which type of distribution typically provides continuous updates rather than fixed major releases?**
    A) Long-term support (LTS) distribution
    B) Stable release distribution
    C) Rolling-release distribution
    D) Minimal distribution

4. **Why are beginner-friendly distributions often recommended for new users?**
    - A) They restrict access to most system features
    - B) They provide easier installation, sensible defaults, and strong community support
    - C) They require advanced technical knowledge to operate
    - D) They prevent software updates

5. **Choosing a distribution is a permanent decision that cannot be changed later.**
    True or False

6. **Why does this book emphasize skills that transfer across different distributions?**
    - A) Because each distribution uses completely different commands
    - B) Because graphical interfaces are identical on all systems
    - C) Because core Linux concepts remain consistent across environments
    - D) Because distributions cannot run the same software

CHAPTER 2 ANSWER KEY

1. **B** — A distribution combines the Linux kernel with software, tools, and configuration into a usable operating system.

2. **True** — Distributions share the kernel but vary in interface, tools, and focus.

3. **C** — Rolling-release distributions deliver updates continuously instead of in large version jumps.

4. **B** — Beginner distributions prioritize usability, stability, and accessible support resources.

5. **False** — Users can switch distributions, and many Linux skills apply across systems.

6. **C** — Fundamental Linux concepts and command-line skills work across different distributions.

CHAPTER 3
Installing Linux

This chapter explains the main ways to install Linux, beginning with virtual machines and physical hardware, and then walks through the common steps used to complete the installation in either environment.

Installing Linux doesn't necessarily mean replacing your current operating system. There are several ways to begin using Linux, each with a different level of commitment and impact on your computer.

At a basic level, installing Linux means loading a Linux distribution so that it can run on a system. That system may be physical hardware, such as a laptop or desktop computer, or a virtual environment that runs inside another operating system. Some installations are temporary and intended for testing, while others are permanent and used for daily work.

Choosing an Installation Path

Before installing Linux, it helps to decide how Linux will run on your system. This choice affects how it interacts with your existing operating system and how it uses your computer's resources.

There are two primary installation paths:

- Installing Linux on physical hardware
- Running Linux inside a virtual machine

When installing Linux on physical hardware, the operating system runs directly on your computer and can be set up in several ways. Linux can be installed alongside an existing operating system, allowing you to choose which system to start when the computer boots. It can also be run from a USB drive without modifying your hard disk, which is useful for testing and exploration.

Running Linux inside a virtual machine allows you to use Linux within a window on your existing operating system. In this case, Linux behaves like a separate computer, but it does not directly control the hardware. This approach avoids disk partitioning and makes it easy to experiment, but it comes with some performance overhead.

Each option has advantages and trade-offs:

- **Physical installation** provides full performance and direct hardware access, but may require disk changes if installed permanently.

- **Virtual machines** are safer for experimentation and learning, but rely on your host system and use additional system resources.

Neither approach is better in all situations. Beginners often start with a virtual machine or a bootable USB to become familiar with Linux before committing to a permanent installation. Others prefer to install Linux directly to experience it as a primary operating system from the start.

What is a Virtual Machine?

A virtual machine is a software-based computer that runs inside another operating system. It allows you to use one operating system while continuing to use your primary system at the same time. For example, you can run Linux inside a window on a Windows or macOS system without replacing or modifying your existing installation.

The operating system inside the virtual machine behaves as if it were running on its own computer. The virtualization software provides virtual hardware such as a processor, memory, storage, and network interface, while the host system manages how physical resources are shared.

Instead of using a separate hard drive, the virtual machine stores its data in large files on your system that act as virtual disks. This makes it easy to create, copy, or remove virtual machines without affecting the rest of your system.

Virtual machines are typically slower than running an operating system directly on physical hardware, but for learning and experimentation this trade-off is usually acceptable.

There are several reasons beginners often choose to start with a virtual machine:

- You can experiment with Linux safely without modifying your main operating system.
- You can test different distributions before committing to one.
- Mistakes can be undone by deleting or restoring the virtual machine.
- You can run Linux alongside your existing system.

- You can access software that runs on a different operating system.

Actions performed inside a virtual machine remain contained within that environment, making it well suited for testing software and practicing new skills without risking unintended changes to your main system.

For these reasons, virtual machines are a popular starting point for learning Linux.

Installing Linux on Windows

On Windows systems, there are several ways to run Linux in a virtualized environment. While these tools differ in complexity and scope, they all allow Linux to run alongside Windows without replacing your existing system.

- **Hyper-V:** A built-in virtualization feature available in Windows Pro, Enterprise, and Education editions. It allows you to create and manage virtual machines without installing third-party software.

- **Windows Subsystem for Linux (WSL):** A lightweight environment that allows Linux command-line tools to run alongside Windows. WSL is useful for development and scripting but does not provide a full Linux desktop environment by default. For this reason, it is not the primary focus of this book.

- **Oracle VirtualBox:** A widely used virtualization tool that supports many operating systems and provides a full virtual machine experience. Because it is accessible, flexible, and beginner-friendly, this book uses VirtualBox for virtual machine installations.

Installing and Configuring VirtualBox

1. Go to **https://www.virtualbox.org/** to download and install VirtualBox.

2. During the installation, you may be prompted to install device software. Click **Install** to allow this.

3. Launch VirtualBox and click on the **New** button in the VirtualBox Manager.

4. Enter a name for your virtual machine, select **Linux** as the type, and choose the appropriate version (e.g., Ubuntu 64-bit) and click **Next**.

5. Choose the amount of RAM to allocate to your virtual machine. A minimum of 2048 MB is recommended for most Linux distributions. Click **Next**.

6. Select **Create a virtual hard disk now** and click **Create**.

7. Choose the hard disk file type (**VDI** is recommended), then click **Next**.

8. Select **Dynamically allocated** and click **Next**.

9. Set the size of the virtual hard disk (at least 20 GB is recommended) and click **Create**.

10. Select your new virtual machine and click **Settings**.

11. Go to **Storage**, click on the empty CD icon, and then click the CD icon on the right side > **Choose a disk file** to choose your Linux ISO file that you downloaded.

12. Click **Start** to boot the virtual machine. Follow the installation instructions for your chosen Linux distribution.

After starting Linux in a virtual machine, continue with the steps in **Completing the Linux Installation**, which apply to both virtual machines and physical systems.

Shutting Down the VM

When you are finished using a virtual machine, avoid closing the window directly. Instead, select **Close** from the menu and choose **Save the machine state**. This preserves the system exactly as it was and allows you to resume your work later without data loss.

Installing Linux on macOS

Installing Linux in a virtual machine on macOS follows the same general process used on Windows. The primary difference is installing VirtualBox on macOS.

1. Download the macOS version of VirtualBox from the official website.

2. Open the downloaded disk image and follow the installation prompts.

3. Once installed, create a new virtual machine and attach your Linux ISO file.

4. Use the same configuration steps outlined in the Windows section to complete the installation.

Installing Linux on Physical Hardware

Installing Linux on physical hardware means running the operating system directly on your computer rather than inside another operating system. In this setup, Linux has direct access to system resources such as the processor, memory, storage, and connected devices.

There are several ways to install Linux on physical hardware. Linux can be installed alongside an existing operating system, allowing you to choose which system to start when the computer boots. It can also be run directly from a USB flash drive without modifying your hard disk, which is useful for testing and exploration.

In this section, the primary focus is on installing Linux using a bootable USB drive. This approach is commonly used for both testing Linux and performing a full installation. It introduces the core concepts used in most Linux installation methods while keeping risk and complexity low.

Step 1: Preparing Installation Media

Before installing Linux, you need a Linux distribution image file, commonly referred to as an ISO file. This file contains everything required to start Linux and begin the installation process.

You chose a Linux distribution in the previous chapter. If not, return to Chapter 2 and choose one that matches your goals and experience level. Most beginner-friendly distributions provide clear download instructions and documentation.

Linux ISO files should be downloaded directly from the official website of the distribution. Using official sources helps ensure that the software is up to date and has not been modified.

To install Linux from a USB drive, you must create bootable installation media. A USB flash drive of at least 8 GB is recommended. Any existing data on the drive will be erased during this process.

This book uses **Ventoy** to prepare the USB drive. Ventoy simplifies the process by allowing one or more Linux ISO files to be copied directly to the USB drive without reformatting it each time.

1. Download the Linux ISO file from the official website of your chosen distribution.

2. Insert the USB flash drive into your computer. Back up any important data on the drive before continuing.

3. Download Ventoy from its official website and install it according to the instructions for your operating system.

4. Launch Ventoy, select the USB drive from the list, and install Ventoy on the drive.

5. After Ventoy has been installed, copy the Linux ISO file to the USB drive. The ISO file does not need to be extracted.

Once the ISO file has been copied, the USB drive is ready to be used.

Step 2: Booting from the USB Drive

To start Linux from the USB drive, the computer must boot from the USB device instead of the internal storage.

Most systems are configured to boot from the internal hard drive by default. You can temporarily override this behavior by using the system's boot menu.

1. Reboot the computer.

2. As the system starts, press the key shown on the splash screen to access the boot menu. Common keys include **F12**, **F10**, **Esc**, or **Delete**, depending on the manufacturer.

3. Select the USB drive from the boot menu and continue.

On Windows 10 or Windows 11 systems, you can also access advanced startup options by holding the **Shift** key while selecting **Restart**, then choosing the option to boot from a USB device.

When the system boots from the USB drive, Ventoy displays a menu listing the available ISO files. Select the Linux distribution you want to start. Linux will now load into a live environment, where you can test the system or proceed with installation.

Completing the Linux Installation

Once Linux has been started from installation media, the remaining steps are largely the same whether you are installing Linux on physical hardware or inside a virtual machine. This section describes the common steps involved in completing the installation and preparing the system for first use. Some steps are optional and depend on your chosen setup, and these are clearly marked.

Step 1: Trying Linux Before Installing (optional)

Testing Linux before installing it is optional but strongly recommended, especially if you are new to Linux or unsure which distribution to choose. Booting from the USB drive allows you to start a live environment where Linux runs without making changes to your system.

When starting your distribution, look for an option such as **Try** rather than Install. This allows you to explore the system, check hardware compatibility, and become familiar with the environment before committing to installation.

Some distributions support persistence in live mode, which allows files to be saved during the session. This can be useful for short-term testing, but it is not a replacement for a full installation.

Step 2: Installing Linux

To begin the installation, select the option to install Linux from the boot menu rather than launching the live environment. The installer will guide you through the process and handle most configuration automatically.

You will be asked to choose basic settings such as language, keyboard layout, and time zone. These choices affect how the system behaves but can be changed later if needed.

Step 3: Creating a User Account

During installation, you will create a user account for the system. This includes your name, a computer name, a username, and a password.

The user account is used to log in and to perform administrative tasks. On most systems, administrative actions require confirmation using your password rather than unrestricted access, which improves system security.

Step 4: Disk Layout and Partitioning (Optional)

If Linux is being installed as the only operating system, disk configuration is typically handled automatically and requires no changes.

If you are installing Linux alongside another operating system, the installer may prompt you to create or adjust disk partitions. A partition is a defined section of the disk used by an operating system to store data.

Many beginner-friendly distributions handle this process automatically. If manual configuration is required, ensure that sufficient disk space is allocated and that the partition is formatted using a Linux-compatible file system such as Ext4.

Step 5: First Boot and Hardware Check

After installation completes, restart the system. On startup, you may see a bootloader menu that allows you to choose which operating system to run. One commonly used bootloader is GNU GRUB.

Once Linux has started, verify that essential hardware such as networking, display output, and input devices are functioning correctly. Most hardware works without additional configuration, but some components, particularly graphics cards, may benefit from installing additional drivers later.

Using the GUI and the Command Line

After installing Linux, you will typically interact with the system using both a graphical user interface (GUI) and the command-line interface (CLI), also known as the shell.

Most Linux distributions include a desktop environment that allows you to navigate files, launch applications, and configure basic settings visually. For new users, the GUI provides a familiar way to explore the system and perform common tasks.

However, the command line offers a powerful and consistent way to interact with Linux across distributions and environments. Many administrative and development tasks can be performed more efficiently using commands than through graphical menus.

Rather than replacing the GUI, the command line complements it. Many users switch between the two depending on the task. As you continue through this book, you will gradually build confidence working with the shell while still using the graphical interface when it is convenient.

Chapter 3 Summary

- Linux can be installed on physical hardware or inside a virtual machine, depending on your goals and system setup.

- Virtual machines provide a safe way to experiment, while physical installations allow Linux to run directly on the system.

- Installation begins from an ISO file, started from a USB drive or attached to a virtual machine.

- Many distributions offer a live environment for testing before installation.

- Although installer interfaces vary, the core steps are similar: creating a user account, configuring storage when required, and completing the first boot.

- Most systems function immediately after installation, though some hardware may require additional drivers.

In the next chapter, you will begin working with the Linux shell, which is the primary way you will interact with the system throughout this book.

CHAPTER 3 QUIZ

Try these questions to check your understanding of the key concepts from this chapter. The answer key is provided on the next page.

1. **Which installation method allows you to use Linux without changing your existing operating system or disk setup?**
    A) Replacing the current operating system
    B) Installing Linux as the only system on the computer
    C) Running Linux in a virtual machine
    D) Removing all existing partitions

2. **A live USB environment allows you to try Linux without permanently installing it.**
    True or False

3. **What is an ISO file in the context of Linux installation?**
    A) A file containing user data backups
    B) A configuration file for hardware drivers
    C) An image file containing the operating system installation media
    D) A compressed archive of system logs

4. Why is it recommended to try Linux in a live environment before installing it?
    A) It improves system performance permanently
    B) It installs drivers automatically without user input
    C) It allows you to test compatibility without making changes to the system
    D) It deletes the existing operating system

5. Booting from a USB drive means the computer starts the operating system from the external device instead of internal storage.
    True or False

6. What is a key advantage of using a virtual machine for learning Linux?
    A) It permanently replaces the host operating system
    B) It allows Linux to run safely inside another operating system
    C) It provides direct control of hardware without restrictions
    D) It prevents the system from shutting down

CHAPTER 3 ANSWER KEY

1. **C** — A virtual machine runs Linux inside your current system without modifying the disk.

2. **True** — A live USB loads Linux into memory so it can be used without installation.

3. **C** — The ISO file contains the complete installation image for the operating system.

4. **C** — A live environment lets you verify hardware support and usability safely.

5. **True** — Booting from USB loads the operating system from the external drive.

6. **B** — A virtual machine provides an isolated environment for safe experimentation.

CHAPTER 4
The Linux Shell

With Linux freshly installed, it's time to begin interacting with your new operating system! While many everyday tasks can be performed using a graphical user interface, Linux also provides a powerful text-based interface accessed through a shell. The shell plays a central role in system administration, automation, and troubleshooting, making it an essential tool to understand.

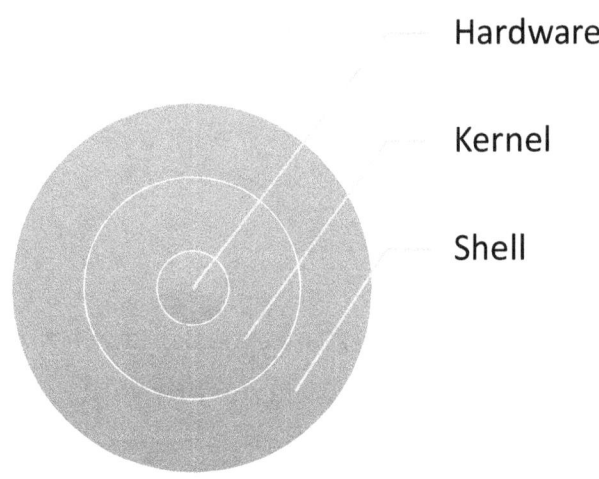

Linux operates in layers. At the core is the **hardware**, managed by the **kernel**, which is responsible for communication between the system and physical components. Above the kernel are user-level programs such as the **shell**, which allow users to issue commands and control the system. This layered design allows users to interact with complex hardware through simple commands. The graphic illustrates this hierarchy and shows how commands flow from the user down through these layers to the components that carry them out.

In this chapter, you will learn what the shell is and how it interacts with the terminal to provide access to the command line. You will explore the different types of shells available in Linux and understand the distinction between the terminal and the shell. You will then learn how to access the shell locally or remotely, develop essential command-line editing skills, and gain a high-level understanding of shell scripting.

What is the Shell?

Computers ultimately operate using binary, with 1s and 0s representing electrical states. If users had to interact with a computer using binary directly, even simple tasks would be extremely time-consuming. The shell exists to remove this complexity and make systems usable by humans.

The shell acts as a translator between human-readable commands and the Linux kernel, which carries out those instructions. By allowing commands to be entered as readable text, the shell lets users work efficiently without needing to understand low-level machine code.

The shell has several key characteristics:

- **User Program:** The shell is a user-level program that provides an environment designed for human interaction with the operating system.

- **Command Interpreter:** The shell interprets commands entered through a command-line interface (CLI) and passes them to the kernel for execution.

- **Automatic:** The shell starts automatically when you open a terminal or log into a system through a text-based session.

- **Works with the Kernel:** Although the shell is not part of the kernel, it works closely with it to run programs, manage files, and perform system tasks.

- **Versatile:** Linux supports multiple shells. While they all perform the same core role, they differ in syntax, features, and built-in functionality.

Types of Shells

When working with Linux, you will encounter different types of shells. A shell is a program that interprets the commands you type and passes them to the operating system for execution. Although many shells exist, most belong to one of two major families: Bourne-style shells and C-style shells.

Although shells differ in syntax, features, and user experience, they all serve the same fundamental purpose: interpreting user commands and enabling interaction with the operating system.

Bourne-Style Shells

The Bourne shell family originated in early Unix systems and forms the foundation of most shells used on Linux today. Bourne-style shells are widely preferred for scripting because of their consistency and compatibility.

- **Bourne Shell (sh):** The original Unix shell. While rarely used interactively today, it remains important as the basis for many modern shells and shell scripts.

- **Bourne Again Shell (bash):** A free and enhanced replacement for sh and the default shell on most Linux distributions. Bash includes features such as command history, tab completion, job control, and powerful scripting capabilities. Because of its widespread availability and extensive documentation, Bash is the primary shell used throughout this book.

- **Zsh (Z Shell):** An advanced Bourne-compatible shell that offers extensive customization, improved tab completion, and optional spelling correction. It is the default shell on modern macOS systems and is popular among advanced users.

- **Fish (Friendly Interactive SHell):** Designed to be easy to use, Fish provides autosuggestions, syntax highlighting, and a simplified configuration process without requiring extensive setup. It is commonly used for interactive work but less often for scripting.

- **Korn Shell (ksh):** A Bourne-compatible shell that introduced several advanced features later adopted by other shells. It is still used in some enterprise and legacy environments.

In modern Linux systems, Bash remains the most widely used shell.

C-Style Shells

C-style shells are named for their syntax, which resembles the C programming language. They are less common on modern Linux systems but may still appear in legacy environments or specialized workflows.

- **C Shell (csh):** Introduced features such as command history and job control earlier than some Bourne-style shells. Despite its historical importance, csh is generally not recommended for scripting due to design limitations.

- **TENEX/TOPS C Shell (tcsh):** An enhanced version of csh that adds command-line editing and filename completion. While still available, it is primarily encountered on older systems.

For beginners, learning Bash is recommended because it is widely available, well documented, and compatible with most Linux environments. Unless otherwise stated, examples in this book assume the Bash shell.

What is the Terminal?

A terminal is a program that provides access to a command-line interface (**CLI**), allowing users to interact with the operating system by entering text-based commands. Through the terminal, users communicate with a shell such as Bash, which interprets those commands and carries them out.

On Linux and macOS systems, a terminal application is typically installed by default. Windows also provides command-line environments, including Command Prompt and PowerShell. Additionally, installing Git for Windows provides access to Git Bash, which offers a terminal experience similar to that found on Linux systems.

Using the terminal, you can perform a wide range of tasks efficiently, such as navigating the file system, creating and managing directories, and executing commands to control and automate system behavior.

Terminal vs Shell

A terminal and a shell are closely related but serve different roles. The terminal is the application that provides the interface where you type commands and view output. The shell is the program running inside that interface that interprets those commands and communicates with the operating system.

In simple terms, the terminal provides the window, and the shell provides the command-processing logic. When you open a terminal, a shell session typically starts automatically, allowing you to interact with the system.

You interact with the shell through the terminal.

Where Commands Come From

Not every command in Linux is a separate program you install. Some commands are built directly into the shell, while others are external utilities stored on the system.

Shell built-ins are part of the shell itself and do not exist as standalone files. Commands such as cd, history, and exit fall into this category.

Many commonly used commands are external programs included with the operating system. Tools such as ls, cp, mv, and grep are separate utilities that the shell runs when you type their names.

Additional commands can be installed later using the package manager. Programs such as git or htop become available only after installation.

From the user's perspective, these differences are mostly invisible. The shell accepts a command name, locates the appropriate implementation, and executes it. Understanding that commands may come from different sources helps explain why some commands are always available while others must be installed.

Gaining Access to the Shell

When interacting with a shell, there are several methods available. The most common ways to access the shell include using a terminal or establishing a secure shell (SSH) connection. Each method comes with different levels of permissions and capabilities.

Typically, you'll find yourself working with **Bash** (Bourne Again SHell), which is the default shell for many Linux distributions. However, you may also encounter other shells, such as Zsh, Fish, or Ksh, each offering unique features and functionalities. Understanding how to access the shell is essential for effective interaction with your operating system.

Terminal Access to the Shell

On Linux, the terminal application is included by default. Open the application menu and look for an app labeled **Terminal**, often found under categories such as System Tools, Utilities, or Accessories. Many systems also allow you to press the **Super (Windows) key** and type "terminal" to search for it.

On Windows, a native Linux shell is not included by default. However, installing Git for Windows provides Git Bash, which offers a Bash environment suitable for practicing Linux commands. After installation, you can launch Git Bash from the Start menu.

A terminal emulator is a program that provides a windowed interface for interacting with a shell. It replaces the physical terminals used in early Unix systems and allows users to work with the command line within a graphical desktop environment. Terminal emulators handle input and output, while the shell processes the commands.

Common terminal emulators on Linux include GNOME Terminal, Konsole, xterm, and lxterminal. Most distributions provide one of these by default, typically labeled simply as "Terminal" in the application menu.

When you open a terminal, it displays a prompt showing that it is ready to accept a command. For a normal user, this prompt usually includes a dollar sign ($). You type your command after the prompt and press Enter to run it. The prompt itself is part of the display and is not typed. Essential Linux commands are introduced in Chapter 5.

Secure Shell Connection

SSH, short for **Secure Shell**, is a network protocol that allows you to securely access and manage remote systems over a network. It encrypts the connection between systems, ensuring that commands, data, and credentials cannot be read by third parties.

Common reasons for using SSH include the following:

- **Encrypted Communication:** SSH encrypts all data transmitted between the client and the remote system. This protects against eavesdropping, man-in-the-middle attacks, and other network-based threats, ensuring that sensitive information such as passwords and files remains protected.

- **Remote System Management:** SSH allows users and administrators to access and manage systems remotely from any location. This makes it possible to perform configuration, troubleshooting, and maintenance tasks without needing physical access to the machine. SSH is widely used to manage servers in data centers and cloud environments.

- **File Transfer and Tunneling:** SSH supports secure file transfer using tools such as **SCP** (Secure Copy Protocol) and **SFTP** (SSH File Transfer Protocol). It can also be used to create encrypted tunnels for other network services, allowing secure access to applications or databases that are not directly exposed to the internet.

To create an SSH connection, two components are required: an **SSH client** and an **SSH server**. The client runs on your local machine and initiates the connection, while the server runs a background service that listens for incoming SSH requests. Once authentication succeeds, an encrypted connection is established between the two systems.

A widely used open-source implementation of SSH is **OpenSSH**. Many Linux distributions include the SSH client by default, but this is not always guaranteed.

To check whether the SSH client is installed on your system, open a terminal and type:

```
ssh
```

If the client is installed, the terminal will display usage information. If the command is not found, you will need to install the OpenSSH client.

On Debian-based systems such as Ubuntu, you can install the client using:

    sudo apt install openssh-client

You will be prompted to enter your user password to authorize the installation.

To accept incoming SSH connections, the remote system must also have the OpenSSH server installed and running. If you have permission to manage the remote system, you can first check whether the SSH service is available by running:

    ssh localhost

If the connection fails, the SSH server may not be installed or running. To install the server component, run:

    sudo apt install openssh-server

After installation, verify that the SSH service is active:

```
sudo systemctl status ssh
```

If the service is running, the system is ready to accept SSH connections. You can now connect to this machine or other remote systems using SSH, provided you have the necessary credentials and permissions.

Installing Bash on Windows

Installing Linux in a virtual machine or on physical hardware provides the full experience, but Bash on Windows offers a convenient way to practice Linux commands without leaving the Windows environment. While not a complete replacement, the skills learned transfer directly to Linux systems.

To install Bash on Windows, you will use the **Git for Windows** installer from https://gitforwindows.org/

1. First, download the **Git for Windows** installer. When you run the installer, click **Run**, and on the next five screens, simply click **Next**.

2. When prompted, choose **Git from the command line and also from 3rd party software**, then click **Next**. This selection ensures you can access Bash via the command line.

3. Click **Next** again to proceed.

4. Select **Checkout Windows-style, commit Unix-style line endings**, and then click **Next**.

5. On the next screen, select the second option: **Use Windows' default console window**, and click **Next**.

6. Click **Next** once more to continue.

7. Once the installation is finished, select **Finish**.

After completing these steps, you should have **Git Bash** available.

Basic Command-Line Editing

When working in the shell, mistakes are normal. Command-line editing shortcuts allow you to quickly correct errors without retyping an entire command. These shortcuts become especially useful as commands grow longer or more complex.

For example, if you type a long command and notice a mistake at the beginning, pressing **Ctrl + A** moves the cursor instantly to the start of the line. This allows you to fix the error without deleting and retyping the whole command.

If you need to add or modify something at the end of a command, **Ctrl + E** moves the cursor directly to the end of the line so you can continue typing immediately.

Bash provides several built-in keyboard shortcuts that make interactive command-line work faster and more efficient. Some commonly used shortcuts include:

- **Ctrl + A** – Move to the beginning of the line
- **Ctrl + E** – Move to the end of the line
- **Ctrl + U** – Clear the line before the cursor
- **Ctrl + K** – Clear the line after the cursor
- **Ctrl + C** – Cancel the current command

Learning these shortcuts improves accuracy and speed, especially when working with longer commands. Over time, they become second nature and significantly reduce the effort required to work in the terminal.

A quick reference of common command-line shortcuts is provided in Appendix C.

Shell Scripting

Shell scripting is a way to automate tasks by grouping multiple shell commands into a single file called a script. Instead of typing the same commands repeatedly, a script allows you to run them all at once. This makes scripting especially useful for routine operations, system maintenance, and administrative tasks.

A shell script is interpreted line by line by a shell such as Bash, executing each command in sequence. Because scripts rely on precise syntax and structure, commands must be written correctly for the shell to understand and carry them out. Even small mistakes can prevent a script from running as intended.

What a Shell Script Looks Like

A shell script is a plain text file containing commands that could otherwise be typed manually into the terminal. Scripts often begin with a special line called a **shebang**, which tells the system which shell should interpret the script.

```
#!/bin/sh
```

The #! sequence instructs the system to use a specific interpreter. In this example, /bin/sh refers to a Bourne-compatible shell available on the system.

After the shebang, you can write the commands you want the shell to execute. For example, a simple script might list the contents of the current directory and save the output to a file:

```
ls -l > filelist.txt
```

The > symbol redirects the command's output to a file instead of displaying it on the screen. If the file does not exist, it is created. If it already exists, its contents are replaced.

This example demonstrates how a script can combine commands and output redirection into a repeatable task.

Running a Shell Script

Once a script has been created, it can be executed by passing it to the shell directly. For example:

```
bash filelist.sh
```

This tells bash to read and execute the commands contained in the script file. For now, it is enough to understand how scripts are run; file permissions and execution methods will be covered in more detail later.

Shell Scripting Concepts (High-Level)

Shell scripts rely on several core concepts that allow them to make decisions and repeat actions. These include:

- Conditional logic, which allows commands to run only when certain conditions are met
- Loops, which repeat commands automatically
- Functions, which group related commands into reusable blocks

Although these capabilities make scripting powerful, they also require precise syntax and careful structure. This book focuses on understanding how commands work and how they can be combined, rather than teaching full scripting techniques.

Chapter 4 Summary

- The shell is the primary interface used to interact with Linux systems.

- Linux supports multiple shells, with Bash being the most common.

- The terminal provides a graphical window for accessing the shell.

- Linux commands may come from different sources, including shell built-ins and external programs.

- The shell can be accessed locally through a terminal or remotely using Secure Shell (SSH) over an encrypted connection.

- Command-line editing shortcuts improve efficiency when working interactively.

- Shell scripting allows commands to be grouped into executable scripts.

Mastering the shell is essential for effective system administration, automation, and troubleshooting in Linux environments.

In the next chapter, you will begin working directly with essential Linux commands that form the foundation of everyday system use.

CHAPTER 4 QUIZ

Try these questions to check your understanding of the key concepts from this chapter. The answer key is provided on the next page.

1. **What is the primary function of the Linux shell?**
    A) To display graphical windows and icons
    B) To interpret commands and communicate with the operating system
    C) To manage hardware resources directly
    D) To replace the kernel during startup

2. **The terminal and the shell refer to the same component of the system.**
    True or False

3. **Which shell is the default on most Linux distributions and is used throughout this book?**
    A) Fish
    B) Zsh
    C) Bash
    D) tcsh

4. **What happens when you press Enter after typing a command in the shell?**

A) The terminal closes
   B) The shell interprets the command and requests the system to execute it
   C) The command is saved for later use
   D) The kernel shuts down the session

5. SSH is commonly used to securely access and manage a system over a network.

   True or False

6. What best describes a shell script?
   A) A graphical tool for managing files
   B) A compiled program written in a programming language
   C) A text file containing a sequence of commands that can be executed together
   D) A configuration file used by the kernel

CHAPTER 4 ANSWER KEY

1. **B** — The shell interprets user commands and passes them to the operating system for execution.

2. **False** — The terminal provides the interface, while the shell processes the commands entered within it.

3. **C** — Bash is the most widely used shell and the one assumed throughout the book.

4. **B** — Pressing Enter submits the command for interpretation and execution by the shell.

5. **True** — SSH provides encrypted remote access to another system across a network.

6. **C** — A shell script automates tasks by running multiple commands from a single file.

CHAPTER 5
Essential Linux Commands

This chapter introduces the core command-line tools used to navigate the system, inspect files, and perform everyday tasks safely from the terminal.

Working effectively with Linux requires understanding how commands interact with the system and what they operate on. In Linux, most tasks revolve around files, directories, and running processes, and commands are the tools used to inspect or manipulate them.

The commands in this chapter focus on exploring and managing files and directories from the terminal. While some examples reference elevated privileges, system configuration, user management, and software installation are covered in later chapters. These tools form the foundation for the command-line work used throughout the rest of this book.

Working in the Terminal

When you open a terminal, you are interacting with a shell, which is a program that accepts commands and passes them to the operating system for execution. Each command is entered at a prompt, which indicates that the shell is ready to receive input.

Most commands operate on files or directories, either by displaying information or by performing an action. Linux is case-sensitive, meaning that files named File.txt and file.txt are treated as different objects. Paying attention to spelling and capitalization is essential when working in the terminal.

The shell prompt typically ends with a symbol such as $, which indicates that you are working as a regular user. Commands entered as a regular user can perform many useful tasks without risking system stability or security. Administrative commands, which require elevated privileges, are introduced later in this book.

Most Linux commands include built-in documentation accessible with the man command. Typing man followed by a command name displays detailed usage information, and pressing the **q** key exits the viewer.

Navigating the File System

Before working with files from the command line, it helps to recall how Linux organizes information.

Linux uses a hierarchical file system that begins at a single top-level directory known as the root directory. All files and directories exist somewhere within this structure. Unlike some operating systems, Linux does not use drive letters. Instead, storage devices and partitions appear as directories within the same tree.

When you use the terminal, you are always working from a specific location in the file system known as the **current working directory**. Many commands operate relative to this location, so the same command can produce different results depending on where you are.

Paths in Linux can be specified in two ways: **absolute path** and **relative path**.

For example, if a file is located at:

    /home/user/Documents/report.txt

This is an absolute path because it starts from the root directory.

If you are already inside the Documents directory, the same file could be referenced using the relative path:

```
report.txt
```

Understanding the difference between these two types of paths is essential for navigating efficiently.

Each user account also has a home directory, which is the default starting location when opening a terminal. Personal files, configuration files, and other user-specific data are typically stored here.

A visual overview of the Linux file system hierarchy is provided in Appendix B for quick reference.

Viewing Your Current Location:

To display the directory you are currently working in, use:

```
pwd
```

This command prints the full path of the current working directory.

Listing Directory Contents:

To view the files and directories in the current location, use:

    ls

By default, this command lists visible files and directories. It does not change your location in the file system.

Wildcards can be used to match multiple files at once. For example, ls *.txt lists all files ending with .txt in the current directory.

Changing Directories:

To move from one directory to another, use:

    cd directory_name

You can use cd with either an absolute path or a relative path. To return to your home directory at any time, run:

    cd

To move up one level in the directory hierarchy, use:

```
cd ..
```

The ~ symbol is a shortcut for your home directory:

```
cd ~
```

This command returns you to your home directory from anywhere in the file system.

Why Navigation Matters

Navigating the file system correctly helps you understand how commands operate on files and directories. Before modifying or deleting files, it is good practice to confirm your current location and inspect directory contents.

Viewing and Inspecting Files

Before modifying files, it is often useful to view their contents or inspect their type. Linux provides several commands that allow you to examine files safely without changing them.

Many configuration files, logs, and documents in Linux are plain text. This makes it possible to inspect them directly from the terminal using simple tools. Other files, such as images or compiled programs, are binary and cannot be meaningfully displayed as text. The commands in this section help you distinguish between these cases.

Viewing File Contents:

To display the contents of a small text file directly in the terminal, use:

```
cat filename
```

This command outputs the entire file at once. It is best used for short files, as longer files can quickly scroll past the screen.

Viewing Files One Screen at a Time:

For larger files, a paging tool is more practical:

```
less filename
```

This command allows you to scroll through a file one screen at a time. You can move forward and backward, search for text, and exit the viewer without modifying the file.

Viewing the Beginning or End of a File:

To view only the first few lines of a file, use:

```
head filename
```

To view the last few lines, use:

```
tail filename
```

These commands are commonly used to inspect configuration files or to check the most recent entries in log files.

Identifying File Types:

Not all files are plain text. To determine the type of a file, use:

```
file filename
```

This command examines the file and reports what kind of data it contains, such as text, an image, or a binary executable. This is especially useful when file extensions are missing or misleading.

Why Read-Only Tools Matter

Read-only commands allow you to examine files and directories without making changes. When learning Linux, it's helpful to inspect files first and understand their contents before editing or removing them.

Creating and Managing Files and Directories

After learning how to navigate the file system and inspect files safely, the next step is creating and managing files and directories. These commands allow you to organize information and make changes to the file system.

Unlike the commands in the previous section, the commands introduced here modify files or directories, so it is important to understand what each command does before using it.

Creating Empty Files:

To create an empty file, use:

```
touch filename
```

This command creates a new file if it does not already exist. If the file already exists, touch updates its timestamp without changing its contents.

Creating Directories:

To create a new directory, use:

```
mkdir directory_name
```

Directories are used to group related files and keep the file system organized. You can create directories inside other directories by specifying a path.

Copying Files and Directories:

To copy a file from one location to another, use:

```
cp source destination
```

This command creates a duplicate of the file at the destination location. To copy an entire directory and its contents, you must include the recursive option:

```
cp -r source_directory destination
```

Moving and Renaming Files:

To move a file or directory, use:

```
mv source destination
```

This command can also be used to rename files. When the source and destination are in the same directory, the file is simply renamed.

Deleting Files and Directories:

To remove a file, use:

```
rm filename
```

To remove an empty directory, use:

```
rmdir directory_name
```

To remove a directory and its contents, use:

```
rm -r directory_name
```

Deleting files and directories from the command line does not move them to a recycle bin. Once removed, the data is usually difficult to recover. Always verify your current location and the target before running removal commands.

Working Safely

Commands that modify the file system should be used deliberately. Listing directory contents and confirming paths before copying, moving, or deleting files helps maintain an organized and predictable workflow.

In the next section, you will learn how to search for files and text using powerful command-line tools.

Finding Files and Content

As systems grow and files accumulate, locating information efficiently becomes important. Linux provides powerful tools for finding files by name and searching for text within files directly from the terminal.

There is an important distinction between **finding files** and **searching file contents**. Some commands locate files based on their name or location, while others search inside files for specific text. Understanding this difference helps you choose the right tool for the task.

Finding Files by Name:

To search for files and directories by name, use:

    find path -name filename

This command searches through the specified path and all of its subdirectories. For example, to search your home directory for a file named notes.txt, you would start the search from your home directory.

The find command is precise and reliable, but it can take longer to run on large directory trees because it searches the file system directly.

Using a File Index:

Some systems provide an indexed search tool that can locate files quickly:

    locate filename

The locate command searches a prebuilt index of files rather than scanning the file system in real time. This makes it very fast, but the index may not always reflect recent changes unless it has been updated.

Not all distributions enable locate by default. Installing and updating tools such as locate is covered in the next chapter on package management.

Searching Inside Files:

To search for text within files, use:

```
grep pattern filename
```

This command scans a single file for lines that match the specified pattern and displays any matches found. It is commonly used to search configuration files, logs, and source code.

You can also search across multiple files at once. For example, the following command searches all files ending with .log in the current directory for lines containing the word "error":

```
grep "error" *.log
```

Techniques for diagnosing problems using system logs are introduced in Chapter 9, Troubleshooting Linux.

Choosing the Right Tool

Each search command serves a different purpose. Use file-name searches when you know what a file is called, and content searches when you are looking for specific information inside files.

Learning how to locate information efficiently is an essential skill when working from the command line.

File Ownership and Permissions

Linux controls access to files and directories through a system of ownership and permissions. Every file and directory has an owner and a group, and each object defines what actions are allowed.

Understanding permissions is essential when working in the command line. Many errors, including "Permission denied," are related to access restrictions rather than system failures.

Viewing File Permissions:

To see file ownership and permissions, use:

```
ls -l
```

This displays detailed information about each file. A typical output might look like:

```
-rw-r--r-- 1 user user  1240 Mar 10  example.txt
```

The first section represents the file type and permissions. The next columns show the owner and the group.

Understanding Permission Symbols:

Permissions are represented by three sets of three characters:

```
rwx rwx rwx
```

They apply to:

- The file owner
- The group
- All other users

Each position represents:

- r — read permission
- w — write permission
- x — execute permission

If a permission is not granted, a dash (-) appears instead.

For example:

```
-rw-r--r--
```

This means:

- The owner can read and write.
- The group can read.
- Others can read.
- No one can execute the file.

The first character in the listing (-) is not a permission. It indicates the file type, which in this case is a *regular file*.

Some file types include:

- - Regular file
- d Directory
- l Symbolic link (*symlink*)

Other letters exist for special system files, but most beginners will mainly encounter regular files and directories.

Changing Permissions with chmod:

Permissions can be modified using the chmod command. A beginner-friendly method uses symbolic notation.

To add execute permission for the owner:

```
chmod u+x filename
```

To remove write permission for the group:

```
chmod g-w filename
```

In symbolic mode:

- u stands for user (owner)
- g stands for group
- o stands for others
- a stands for all

This approach is easier to understand than numeric mode and is recommended for beginners.

Changing Ownership with chown:

File ownership can be changed using the chown command. Because ownership affects access rights at the system level, administrative privileges are usually required.

Some commands that modify system settings require elevated access. In such cases, the command is preceded by sudo. The concept of sudo is explained in detail in Chapter 7, Users and Privileges.

```
sudo chown username filename
```

To change both owner and group:

```
sudo chown username:groupname filename
```

Why Permissions Matter

Permissions protect system files and prevent accidental modification. They also allow multiple users to share a system securely.

If you encounter a "Permission denied" message, it usually means that your user account does not have the required access to that file or directory.

Inspecting the System and Its Activity

In addition to working with files and directories, it is often useful to view information about the system itself. Linux provides several commands that display details about the operating system, hardware, resource usage, and running programs.

These commands allow you to inspect the system safely and understand what is running, how resources are being used, and what environment you are working in.

Viewing System and Kernel Information:

To display basic information about the system and kernel, use:

```
uname
```

This command reports details about the system, such as the kernel name and version. It is commonly used to confirm the type of system you are running.

Viewing Disk Usage:

To see how much disk space is used and available, use:

```
df -h
```

This command displays disk usage information for mounted file systems. It helps you understand storage availability without modifying any data.

Viewing Directory Sizes:

To check the size of a directory and its contents, use:

    du -h

This command reports how much space files and directories occupy. It is useful for identifying large folders when managing storage. The -h option displays sizes in a human-readable format.

Viewing Running Processes:

In Linux, a running program is called a process. Each process is assigned a unique Process ID (PID). To display information about currently running processes, use:

    ps aux

This command shows a snapshot of active processes on the system.

Monitoring System Activity:

To view system activity in real time, use:

    top

This command displays an updating list of processes and resource usage, such as CPU and memory consumption.

Stopping an Unresponsive Process:

If a program becomes unresponsive, it can be stopped using the kill command followed by its Process ID (PID):

    kill PID

For example:

    kill 1234

This sends a termination signal to the process, allowing the program to exit.

Why Observation Comes First

Learning how to observe the system builds confidence and improves your understanding of how Linux works. By checking system activity and resource usage, you gain insight into what the system is doing and how commands interact with it.

Using Pipes to Combine Commands

In Linux, commands can be connected so that the output of one command becomes the input of another. This is done using a pipe, represented by the vertical bar character (|).

A pipe allows you to build more powerful operations by combining simple tools. Instead of saving output to a file and processing it separately, the data flows directly between commands.

For example:

```
ls -l | less
```

Here, the detailed file listing produced by ls -l is sent to less, which displays the output one screen at a time.

Another example:

```
ps aux | grep ssh
```

This command lists running processes and then filters the results to show only entries containing the word "ssh".

Pipes are especially powerful when working with commands that produce large amounts of output.

Chapter 5 Summary

- The terminal provides a direct way to interact with the Linux system using commands.

- Navigating the file system relies on understanding directories, paths, and your current location.

- Linux includes powerful tools for inspecting files and searching for information without modifying data.

- Before changing files or directories, it is good practice to confirm your location and examine existing data.

- Every file and directory has an owner and defined permissions that control who can read, write, or execute it.

- File ownership and permissions can be inspected and modified using tools such as ls -l, chmod, and chown.

- Pipes allow simple commands to be combined into more powerful workflows.

Understanding how commands and permissions work together will help you use the Linux system confidently and prepare you for managing software and privileges in the chapters ahead.

In the next chapter, you will learn how Linux installs and manages software using package managers.

CHAPTER 5 QUIZ

Try these questions to check your understanding of the key concepts from this chapter. The answer key is provided on the next page.

1. What command displays the full path of your current working directory?
    - A) ls
    - B) pwd
    - C) cd
    - D) dir

2. Linux file and directory names are case-sensitive.
    True or False

3. Which command is used to change from one directory to another?
    - A) mv
    - B) ls
    - C) cd
    - D) cp

4. Which command is most suitable for viewing a long text file one screen at a time without modifying it?

A) cat
B) less
C) touch
D) rm

5. Removing a file with the rm command typically deletes it permanently rather than sending it to a recycle bin.
   True or False

6. What is the purpose of a pipe (|) in a command such as **ps aux | grep ssh**?
   A) To run commands at the same time on different systems
   B) To save output directly to a file
   C) To send the output of one command as input to another
   D) To grant administrative privileges

CHAPTER 5 ANSWER KEY

1. **B** — The pwd command prints the absolute path of the current working directory.

2. **True** — Linux treats names like File.txt and file.txt as different files.

3. **C** — The cd command changes the current working directory.

4. **B** — The less command allows safe scrolling through large files without editing them.

5. **True** — rm usually removes files permanently unless special recovery tools are used.

6. **C** — A pipe passes the output of one command directly into another command for further processing.

CHAPTER 6
Package Management

This chapter explains how Linux installs, updates, and removes software using a package manager.

In Linux, most software is distributed as packages rather than standalone installers. A package contains the program itself along with information about what it requires to run correctly. The package manager handles downloading these packages, resolving dependencies, and keeping installed software up to date.

Using a package manager provides a consistent and reliable way to manage software across the system. Instead of searching the web for installers, you work with a trusted collection of software maintained by the distribution.

The focus of this chapter is on the everyday tasks involved in managing software from the command line. More advanced configuration and troubleshooting tasks are covered later in the book.

What is Package Management

In Linux, software is managed through a centralized system known as a package manager. Instead of downloading individual installers from different websites, software is installed from trusted collections called repositories.

A **package** contains a program along with the information needed for it to work correctly, such as libraries or supporting components. These supporting components are known as **dependencies**. The package manager automatically handles these dependencies, ensuring that everything required by a program is installed together.

This approach provides consistency across the system. Installed software can be updated, removed, or upgraded using the same set of tools, and updates are applied in a controlled and predictable way. The package manager also helps keep software compatible with the rest of the system.

By using a package manager, Linux reduces the risk of conflicting software versions and simplifies long-term maintenance. Understanding this model is essential before learning the commands used to manage packages from the terminal.

GUI vs CLI Package Management

Many Linux distributions provide graphical tools for installing and updating software. These tools allow users to browse available applications, install programs with a few clicks, and apply updates through a familiar interface.

While graphical tools are convenient, this book focuses on managing software from the command line. Using the CLI provides clearer feedback, greater consistency across systems, and a better understanding of what changes are being made. Regardless of whether a graphical tool or the terminal is used, the same package management system operates underneath.

In the sections that follow, you will learn how to manage software using the command-line package manager commonly found on Debian-based systems.

Introducing APT

On Debian-based Linux distributions, software is managed using a package manager called **APT** (Advanced Package Tool). APT is responsible for locating software, downloading packages, resolving dependencies, and keeping installed programs up to date.

APT works with **repositories**, which are curated collections of software maintained by the distribution. These repositories act as trusted sources. When you install or update software, APT retrieves packages from these sources rather than from random websites. This helps ensure that software is compatible with your system and receives updates alongside the rest of the operating system.

The package manager keeps track of what is installed on your system and what each program depends on. When software is added or removed, APT automatically handles any related components that are required or no longer needed. This reduces conflicts and simplifies system maintenance.

For everyday use, you interact with APT through a small set of commands that handle the most common software management tasks. Those commands are introduced in the next section.

Core APT Commands

Once you understand what APT does, you can begin using it to manage software from the terminal. In normal day-to-day use, only a small set of commands is required.

These commands are typically run from the terminal and may require administrative privileges. Administrative access is usually provided through a tool called sudo, which is introduced in the next chapter.

Refreshing Package Information:

Before installing or upgrading software, it is good practice to refresh the local package list:

    apt update

This command downloads the latest package information from the configured repositories and updates the system's local database. It does not install, remove, or change any software. You can think of this step as refreshing a catalog so the system knows which versions are currently available.

Upgrading Installed Software:

To apply available updates to installed packages, use:

    apt upgrade

This command installs newer versions of packages that are already present on the system, using the information retrieved by apt update. It upgrades software while preserving existing configuration.

If this command is run without first refreshing the package list, only updates known to the system's existing package database will be applied, which may not include the newest available versions.

Searching for Software:

To search for available software by name or description, use:

    apt search keyword

This command helps you discover packages related to a specific task or program.

Installing Software:

To install a package, use:

    apt install package_name

For example, to install the text editor **nano**, you would run:

    apt install nano

APT automatically downloads the package along with any required dependencies. Before proceeding, it displays a summary of what will be installed and asks for confirmation.

Listing Installed Packages:

To view a list of software packages currently installed on the system, use:

```
apt list --installed
```

This command displays all installed packages known to the package manager. Because the list can be long, it is most useful when you want to confirm whether a specific package is installed before attempting to remove it.

The output shows package names exactly as they are recognized by APT. Using the correct package name is important when removing software.

Removing Software:

To remove an installed package, use:

```
apt remove package_name
```

This command removes the specified software while leaving its configuration files intact. Retaining configuration files can be useful if you plan to reinstall the program later.

To remove a package along with its configuration files, use:

    apt purge package_name

This performs a more complete removal and is useful when you want a clean reinstall or to eliminate all traces of the software.

When software is installed, additional packages may be added automatically to satisfy dependencies. After the main program is removed, these supporting packages may no longer be required.

To remove packages that were installed automatically and are no longer needed, use:

    apt autoremove

APT will display the packages it intends to remove and ask for confirmation before proceeding. Running this command periodically helps keep the system clean and reduces wasted disk space.

Understanding Confirmation Prompts

When installing or removing software, APT displays a summary of the actions it will take and asks for confirmation. Reading this information carefully helps prevent unintended changes.

In the next section, you will learn a few practical habits that make software management safer and more predictable over time.

Good Habits for Managing Software

Managing software responsibly helps keep a Linux system stable, secure, and easy to maintain. Developing a few good habits early can prevent many common problems later.

It is good practice to refresh package information regularly before installing or upgrading software. This ensures that the package manager is working with up-to-date information from the repositories.

Installing software from trusted repositories reduces the risk of compatibility issues and security problems. In most cases, repositories are managed automatically by the system and do not require manual changes. Situations where repository configuration needs attention are discussed later in the book.

Removing software you no longer use helps keep the system clean. Unused packages can take up disk space and introduce unnecessary complexity over time.

Before confirming an installation or removal, take a moment to read the summary provided by the package manager. This summary shows what will be installed, upgraded, or removed and helps prevent unintended changes.

Package management tasks typically require administrative privileges. Understanding when elevated permissions are needed, and why, is an important part of working safely with Linux. This topic is explored in more detail in the next chapter.

Chapter 6 Summary

- Linux manages software using packages obtained from trusted repositories rather than individual downloads.

- A package manager automates installation, removal, updates, and dependency handling, ensuring software works correctly with the system.

- Debian-based systems use APT to manage software from the command line.

- Refreshing the package list allows the system to retrieve the latest information about available software before installing or upgrading packages.

- Upgrading software installs newer versions of already installed packages while preserving existing configuration.

- Removing software can leave configuration files and automatically installed dependencies behind, which can be cleaned up when no longer needed.

- A small set of core commands covers most everyday software management tasks.

In the next chapter, you will learn how Linux controls administrative access and why elevated privileges should be used carefully.

CHAPTER 6 QUIZ

Try these questions to check your understanding of the key concepts from this chapter. The answer key is provided on the next page.

1. **What is the primary role of a package manager in Linux?**
    A) To control hardware resources
    B) To install, update, and remove software while managing dependencies
    C) To manage user accounts
    D) To monitor system performance

2. **Which command refreshes the system's package information from repositories?**
    A) apt upgrade
    B) apt install
    C) apt update
    D) apt remove

3. **Running apt upgrade installs newer versions of software that is already installed.**
    True or False

4. Which command removes a package but leaves its configuration files on the system?

    A) apt purge
    B) apt remove
    C) apt autoremove
    D) apt update

5. What is the purpose of apt autoremove?

    A) To remove software installed manually by the user
    B) To remove unused packages that were installed automatically as dependencies
    C) To reinstall broken packages
    D) To upgrade outdated software

6. Why should you carefully read the confirmation prompt shown by APT before proceeding?

    A) It displays system hardware details
    B) It confirms your login credentials
    C) It summarizes the changes that will be made to the system
    D) It shows available desktop environments

CHAPTER 6 ANSWER KEY

1. **B** — A package manager installs, updates, and removes software while automatically handling dependencies.

2. **C** — The apt update command refreshes the local package database with the latest information.

3. **True** — apt upgrade installs newer versions of packages already present on the system.

4. **B** — apt remove uninstalls the program but keeps configuration files for possible future use.

5. **B** — apt autoremove deletes dependencies that were installed automatically and are no longer needed.

6. **C** — The confirmation prompt lists what will be installed, upgraded, or removed before changes occur.

CHAPTER 7
Users and Privileges

In the previous chapters, you learned how to work with Linux as a regular user, installing software and interacting with the system from the command line. You also saw how files are protected using ownership and permissions, and how commands such as chmod and chown control access to files and directories. This chapter introduces how Linux controls access to system-wide actions and protects itself from accidental or unauthorized changes.

Linux is a multi-user operating system. Not all actions are treated equally, and some tasks require elevated privileges because they affect the entire system. Understanding these boundaries helps explain why certain commands behave differently and why Linux enforces a clear separation between users and administrative control.

This chapter explains when elevated access is required, how it is granted, and why it should be used carefully.

Types of Linux Accounts

Every action performed on the system is associated with a specific user account, and different accounts are granted different levels of access. Understanding these distinctions is essential before exploring how elevated privileges are granted and controlled.

Linux supports several account types, but three are fundamental to how permissions and security work: the **root user**, **normal user**, and **system user**. These roles define who can make system-wide changes, who can perform everyday tasks, and how background services operate.

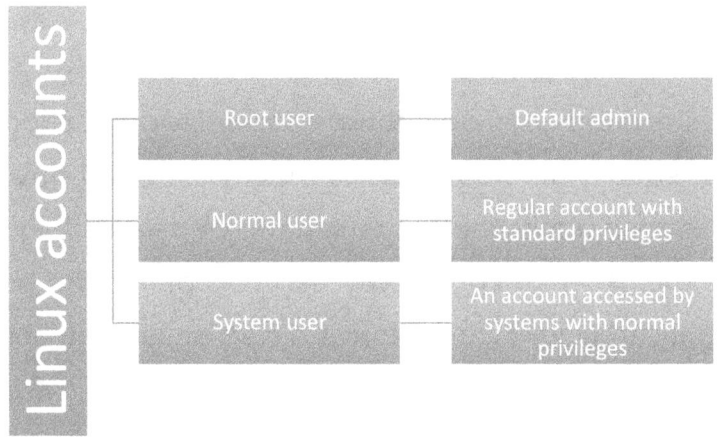

Root User

The root user, often referred to as the **superuser**, is the primary administrative account on a Linux system. This account has unrestricted access to all files, processes, and system settings. With root privileges, any command can be executed without additional approval. On most Linux systems, when working directly as the root user, the shell prompt typically uses the # symbol instead of $, indicating elevated privileges.

Because of this unrestricted power, the root account is typically used only for system setup, maintenance, and recovery tasks. Linux assumes that actions performed as root are intentional. There are no built-in safeguards to prevent destructive commands, and accidental changes can result in serious or irreversible system damage if backups are not available.

On many modern Linux systems, direct login as the root user is disabled by default, and administrative tasks are performed using sudo instead. For this reason, routine tasks are normally performed using a non-privileged account. Root access is reserved for actions that require full system control, such as modifying system files, managing user permissions, repairing the system, or installing software that affects core components.

Normal User

A normal user account represents a person using the system. Each normal user has a dedicated home directory, a login shell, and a unique user identification number (UID) assigned during account creation.

Normal users do not have administrative privileges by default. They can access their own files and any system resources that are not explicitly restricted, but they cannot modify system-wide settings or protected directories.

On personal systems, it is common to work primarily as a normal user and temporarily elevate privileges only when necessary. This separation helps protect the system from accidental changes and limits the impact of mistakes made during everyday use.

System User

System users are accounts created for software and background services rather than for human interaction. These accounts are used by processes such as network services, schedulers, and system daemons that need limited access to specific resources. For example, a web server may run under its own system user account so it can access only the files and resources required for its operation.

Although system users share many characteristics with normal users, they typically do not have login shells or home directories intended for interactive use. Their purpose is organizational and security-related, allowing the system to isolate services and restrict their access.

System accounts are usually created automatically during installation or when software is added. Modifying or removing these accounts is not recommended, as doing so can disrupt essential system functionality.

Sudo

Linux restricts access to system-wide actions by default. Tasks that affect the entire system require elevated privileges to prevent accidental or unauthorized changes. Rather than working permanently as the root user, Linux provides a controlled method for temporarily raising permissions using sudo. The name sudo derives from "superuser do," meaning execute this command with superuser privileges.

The sudo command allows an authorized user to run a single command with administrative privileges. Instead of switching fully to the root account, sudo grants elevated access only for the duration of that specific command. Once the command completes, the user returns to normal privilege level.

When using sudo, the system prompts for the current user's password, not the root password. This confirms the identity of the person requesting elevated access and provides an additional layer of accountability. After authentication, sudo temporarily remembers your credentials, allowing subsequent administrative commands to run without re-entering the password. After a short period of inactivity, elevated privileges expire automatically.

This design encourages safer system use. Everyday tasks are performed as a normal user, while administrative actions are deliberate and clearly separated from routine work.

Using sudo

To run a command with elevated privileges, prefix it with sudo:

```
sudo command
```

Only users who have been granted permission can use sudo. On many personal Linux systems, the first user created during installation is automatically allowed to run administrative commands using sudo.

In multi-user environments, sudo can be configured to grant specific administrative permissions to selected users rather than giving full system access. This flexibility allows administrators to control precisely who can perform certain tasks.

Further details are provided in the **Managing sudo Permissions** section.

su and sudo

Linux provides more than one way to access elevated privileges. In addition to sudo, there is another command called su, which stands for substitute user.

The su command allows you to switch from your current user account to another account, most commonly the root user. When switching to root using su, you are effectively operating as the root user until you exit the session.

```
su
```

If successful, the shell changes to reflect the new user context. When switching to root, the prompt typically changes to #, indicating full administrative privileges.

Unlike sudo, which grants elevated access for a single command, su opens a new shell session under a different user account. This means that every command entered afterward runs with that account's permissions until the session is closed.

Differences Between su and sudo

While both commands provide access to elevated privileges, they serve different purposes:

- sudo runs a single command with elevated privileges.
- su switches to another user account and remains in that account until you exit.
- sudo typically requires your own password.
- su requires the target user's password, often the root password.

Because sudo limits elevation to individual commands, it is generally considered safer for everyday administrative tasks. For this reason, many modern Linux distributions rely primarily on sudo and disable direct root login by default.

When to Use su?

The su command is more commonly used in multi-user or administrative environments where switching between accounts is necessary. For most personal systems, sudo is the preferred method for performing administrative tasks.

Understanding both commands helps clarify how Linux manages identity and privileges. In practice, you will likely encounter sudo more frequently on modern systems.

Managing sudo Permissions

The behavior of sudo is controlled by a configuration file known as the *sudoers file*. This file defines which users or groups are allowed to run commands with elevated privileges and under what conditions.

On most systems, administrative access through sudo is granted by adding a user to a specific group during installation. For example, Debian-based systems typically use the sudo group to manage this access. Users who belong to this group can run administrative commands using sudo.

Although it's possible to edit the sudoers file directly, doing so incorrectly can prevent administrative access altogether. For this reason, Linux provides a tool called visudo, which safely edits the configuration file and checks for syntax errors before saving changes.

In most personal or single-user environments, the default configuration is sufficient for everyday administrative tasks. In larger or shared systems, administrators may adjust these settings to match organizational requirements.

Creating and Managing Users

Linux is designed as a multi-user operating system. Even on a personal machine, there may be valid reasons to create additional accounts, such as separating work and personal environments or setting up accounts for family members. In professional or enterprise environments, managing user accounts is essential for controlling access, enforcing security policies, and maintaining system integrity.

User management in Linux is performed from the command line and requires administrative privileges.

Creating a New User:

To create a new user account, use:

```
sudo adduser username
```

This command:

- Creates a new user account
- Assigns a unique user ID (UID)
- Creates a home directory
- Prompts you to set a password

During the process, you may be asked to enter optional information such as a full name or contact details. These fields can be left blank if not needed.

After creation, the new user can log in and will have a private home directory.

Changing a Password:

To change your own password, use:

```
passwd
```

To change the password of another user, run:

```
sudo passwd username
```

You will be prompted to enter and confirm the new password. This command is commonly used when resetting access for another account.

Adding a User to the sudo Group:

If you want a user to have administrative privileges, you can add them to the sudo group:

```
sudo usermod -aG sudo username
```

The -aG option appends the user to the specified group without removing existing group memberships.

After running this command, the user must log out and log back in for the changes to take effect.

Not every user should be granted administrative privileges. It is good practice to limit sudo access to trusted accounts.

Viewing User and Group Information:

To see which groups a user belongs to, use:

```
groups username
```

For more detailed information, including the user ID and group ID, use:

```
id username
```

These commands help verify whether a user has administrative privileges.

Removing a User (Optional):

If an account is no longer needed, it can be removed:

```
sudo deluser username
```

To remove the user and their home directory:

```
sudo deluser --remove-home username
```

Be cautious when deleting users, as removing the home directory permanently deletes the associated files.

If you run a command and receive a permission error because you forgot to use sudo, you do not need to retype the command. Bash allows you to repeat the previous command using !!.

```
sudo !!
```

This reruns the previous command with administrative privileges.

Chapter 7 Summary

- Linux is a multi-user operating system built around clearly defined user accounts and privilege levels, allowing multiple users to share the same system securely.

- The root user has unrestricted control over the system, while normal users operate with limited permissions to reduce the risk of accidental or harmful changes.

- The sudo command allows temporary administrative access for a single command, reducing the need to log in directly as root.

- The su command switches between user accounts and can provide persistent elevated access when required.

- Administrative permissions are managed through group membership and configuration settings, which determine what actions a user is allowed to perform.

- User accounts can be created, modified, and removed from the command line using administrative privileges.

Understanding how users and privileges work helps you maintain both flexibility and security as you continue exploring more advanced aspects of the Linux system.

In the next chapter, you will learn how Linux systems connect to networks and how to manage basic network settings from the command line.

CHAPTER 7 QUIZ

Try these questions to check your understanding of the key concepts from this chapter. The answer key is provided on the next page.

1. **Why does Linux restrict certain actions to users with elevated privileges?**
    A) To improve graphical performance
    B) To prevent accidental or unauthorized system-wide changes
    C) To reduce disk usage
    D) To limit the number of installed programs

2. **The root user has unrestricted access to all files, processes, and system settings.**
    True or False

3. **What is the main purpose of the sudo command?**
    A) To permanently switch to the root account
    B) To run a single command with administrative privileges
    C) To create a new user account
    D) To monitor system processes

4. Unlike sudo, the su command switches to another user account and remains in that context until you exit.

    True or False

5. Which command is commonly used to create a new user account on a Debian-based system?
    A) usercreate username
    B) adduser username
    C) newuser username
    D) mkuser username

6. Why is it recommended to limit which users have administrative privileges?
    A) To reduce network traffic
    B) To improve system boot time
    C) To maintain system security and prevent misuse
    D) To simplify file organization

CHAPTER 7 ANSWER KEY

1. **B** — Elevated privileges protect the system from accidental or unauthorized changes that affect all users.

2. **True** — The root account has full control over files, processes, and system settings.

3. **B** — sudo grants temporary administrative access for a single command rather than a full session.

4. **True** — su opens a new shell under another user account until the session is closed.

5. **B** — The adduser command creates a new user account and associated settings.

6. **C** — Restricting administrative access reduces the risk of accidental damage or security issues.

CHAPTER 8
Networking

Modern Linux systems rely on network connectivity for software updates, remote access, file transfers, and communication with other systems. Understanding how networking works in Linux allows you to inspect connections, diagnose common issues, and gain insight into how data moves between devices.

This chapter introduces the fundamental networking concepts relevant to everyday Linux use. You will learn how Linux represents network interfaces, how IP addresses and routing function, and how to test connectivity from the command line.

The focus remains practical and observational. Rather than configuring complex network infrastructure, you will learn how to examine your system's network state, verify connectivity, and understand the protocols that make communication possible. These skills provide a foundation for both everyday troubleshooting and more advanced system administration work.

How Linux Connects to a Network

When a Linux system connects to a network, it does so through a network interface. A network interface may be a physical device, such as an Ethernet card or wireless adapter, or a virtual interface created by the system.

Each interface can be assigned an IP address. An IP address uniquely identifies a device on a network and allows it to send and receive data. Without a valid IP address, a system cannot communicate beyond itself.

In addition to an IP address, most systems use a default gateway. The default gateway is the device that forwards traffic from your local network to other networks, including the internet. When your system sends data to an address outside its local network, it passes the data to this gateway.

Linux provides command-line tools that allow you to inspect this configuration safely.

To view network interfaces and their assigned addresses, use:

```
ip addr
```

This command displays all network interfaces, along with their IP addresses and operational status.

To view routing information, including the default gateway, use:

    ip route

This command shows how your system determines where to send outgoing network traffic.

By examining this information, you can understand how your system is connected and where data is being directed.

Testing Connectivity

After inspecting your network configuration, the next step is verifying that your system can communicate with other devices. Linux provides simple command-line tools that allow you to test connectivity safely.

The most commonly used tool is ping.

    ping 8.8.8.8

The ping command sends small test packets to a destination and waits for a reply. If the destination responds, your system displays timing information for each reply. This confirms that basic network communication is functioning.

You can also test connectivity to a domain name:

    ping example.com

If this works, it confirms both network connectivity and proper name resolution.

To stop ping, press: **Ctrl + C**

The summary displayed at the end shows how many packets were sent and received.

If ping reports that the network is unreachable, your system may not have a valid IP address or default route configured. If it reports that the host cannot be resolved, the issue may be related to DNS configuration.

To see the path traffic takes to reach a destination, use:

    traceroute example.com

This command displays each intermediate device (or "hop") between your system and the destination. It can help identify where communication delays or failures occur.

If traceroute is not installed, some systems provide:

    tracepath example.com

These tools allow you to verify connectivity and observe how traffic flows across networks without making any changes to the system.

Name Resolution and DNS

When you connect to a remote system using a domain name, your system must translate that name into an IP address. This process is called name resolution.

For example:

    ping example.com

Before sending network packets, Linux queries a Domain Name System (DNS) server to determine the IP address associated with example.com.

DNS servers used by the system are typically defined in:

/etc/resolv.conf

To view this file:

cat /etc/resolv.conf

The file usually contains one or more lines beginning with:

nameserver

Each entry specifies the IP address of a DNS server the system can use for name resolution.

Linux also supports local hostname definitions in:

/etc/hosts

To view its contents:

cat /etc/hosts

Entries in this file allow specific hostnames to be mapped directly to IP addresses on the local system.

Understanding how DNS is configured helps you interpret how your system translates domain names into reachable addresses.

Viewing Network Activity and Open Connections

In addition to testing connectivity, Linux allows you to inspect active network connections and listening services. This provides visibility into which programs are communicating over the network.

Modern Linux systems use the ss command to display socket information.

To view active connections, use:

```
ss
```

This command displays established connections along with source and destination addresses.

To view listening services, use:

```
ss -l
```

This shows programs that are waiting for incoming connections.

To display additional details, including numeric addresses and port numbers, use:

```
ss -tuln
```

In this command:

- -t displays TCP connections
- -u displays UDP connections
- -l shows listening sockets
- -n prevents name resolution and displays numeric output

You may also encounter the netstat command on older systems:

```
netstat
```

While still available on some distributions, netstat has largely been replaced by ss in modern Linux environments.

Understanding Ports

Network communication uses ports to identify specific services on a system. An IP address identifies a device, while a port identifies a particular service or application running on that device.

For example:

- Web servers commonly use port 80 (HTTP) or 443 (HTTPS).
- Secure Shell (SSH) typically uses port 22.

By examining active connections and listening services, you can better understand how your system communicates with other devices.

Understanding Core Internet Protocols

When your system communicates over a network, it relies on standardized protocols. These protocols define how data is formatted, transmitted, and received between devices.

Earlier in this chapter, you used commands such as ping, ss, and ip route. These tools reveal how your system participates in network communication. The protocols described here explain what happens beneath those commands.

IPv4 and IPv6

IP (Internet Protocol) is responsible for addressing and routing data between systems.

Most networks still use IPv4 addresses, which are written as four numbers separated by dots, such as:

```
192.168.1.10
```

Modern systems also support IPv6, which uses a much larger address space and appears in hexadecimal format, for example:

```
2001:db8::1
```

IPv6 was introduced to address the limited number of available IPv4 addresses and to support the growing number of internet-connected devices.

When you run:

```
ip addr
```

you may see both IPv4 and IPv6 addresses assigned to the same interface.

TCP and UDP

Most application-level communication relies on either TCP or UDP.

TCP (Transmission Control Protocol) provides reliable communication. It ensures that data arrives in order and retransmits lost packets when necessary. Web browsing and secure remote access commonly use TCP.

UDP (User Datagram Protocol) prioritizes speed over reliability. It sends data without guaranteeing delivery, making it suitable for applications such as streaming or online gaming where low latency is more important than perfect accuracy.

When you used:

```
ss -tuln
```

you were viewing active TCP and UDP sockets on your system.

A Layered Approach

Network communication follows a layered model. At a high level:

- **Application Layer:** Generates data for communication (for example, a web browser request)

- **Transport Layer (TCP / UDP):** Manages delivery, reliability, and port identification

- **Internet Layer (IP):** Handles addressing and routing between networks

- **Network Interface:** Transmits data across the physical or wireless connection

Understanding this layered structure helps you interpret how commands and services interact within the system.

Routing and Network Roles

Earlier in this chapter, you viewed routing information using:

```
ip route
```

Routing determines how your system forwards outgoing network traffic. If a destination is within the local network, data is sent directly. If the destination is outside the local network, traffic is sent to the default gateway.

Routers are devices that connect multiple networks and determine how traffic moves between them. In most home or office environments, the router is also responsible for:

- Assigning IP addresses through DHCP

- Translating private addresses to public ones using Network Address Translation (NAT)
- Acting as a firewall

Network Address Translation (NAT)

Most local networks use private IP address ranges that are not directly accessible from the internet. NAT allows multiple devices within a private network to share a single public IP address.

When traffic leaves your local network, the router replaces the private source address with its public address. Responses are then mapped back to the correct internal device.

You do not typically configure NAT directly on a desktop Linux system, but understanding its role helps explain why internal addresses differ from public-facing ones.

Firewalls

A firewall controls which incoming or outgoing connections are allowed. Many Linux systems include firewall software, and most routers also perform basic firewall functions.

While firewall configuration is beyond the scope of this chapter, it is useful to recognize that blocked traffic may be influenced by firewall rules.

Linux as a Network Participant

In everyday use, a Linux system functions as a network client. It requests resources, connects to remote services, and exchanges data.

However, Linux can also serve as a:

- Web server
- File server
- Router
- Firewall

These roles require additional configuration and are typically part of system administration rather than basic usage. The tools introduced in this chapter provide the foundational understanding needed for those more advanced scenarios.

Networking in Context

Networking may seem complex at first, but much of it becomes clearer when viewed from the perspective of your own system. Linux exposes its network state transparently, allowing you to inspect interfaces, addresses, routes, and active connections directly from the command line.

Rather than memorizing protocol definitions, focus on observing how your system behaves. When you view an interface, test connectivity, or examine open sockets, you are seeing different aspects of the same communication process. The layered structure of networking exists to organize that communication in a predictable way.

As you continue working with Linux, these tools will become familiar reference points. They provide insight into how your system interacts with other devices and services, forming an essential foundation for more advanced system administration tasks.

Chapter Summary

- Linux connects to networks through network interfaces that are assigned IP addresses and routing information.

- The ip addr command displays network interfaces and their assigned addresses, while ip route shows how outgoing traffic is directed.

- The ping command tests basic connectivity between systems, and traceroute or tracepath reveals the path traffic takes across networks.

- Domain Name System (DNS) servers translate domain names into IP addresses, and Linux stores DNS configuration in files such as /etc/resolv.conf and /etc/hosts.

- The ss command displays active connections and listening services, allowing you to observe how programs communicate over the network.

- Network communication relies on layered protocols, including TCP and UDP for transport and IP for addressing and routing.

- Concepts such as routing, Network Address Translation (NAT), and firewalls help explain how traffic moves between local and external networks.

Understanding these foundational networking tools and concepts helps you interpret system behavior and prepares you for troubleshooting in the next chapter.

CHAPTER 8 QUIZ

Try these questions to check your understanding of the key concepts from this chapter. The answer key is provided on the next page.

1. What is the purpose of an IP address on a network?
    A) To identify a specific file on a system
    B) To uniquely identify a device so it can send and receive data
    C) To encrypt network traffic
    D) To replace the need for a router

2. The default gateway is used to forward traffic from a local network to other networks.
    True or False

3. Which command displays network interfaces and their assigned IP addresses?
    A) ip route
    B) ss
    C) ip addr
    D) traceroute

4. What does the ping command primarily test?
    A) Disk performance

B) System memory usage
C) Basic network connectivity
D) File transfer speed

5. **Domain names must be translated into IP addresses before communication can occur.**

    True or False

6. **What is the main purpose of the ss command?**
    A) To configure wireless networks
    B) To display active network connections and listening services
    C) To assign IP addresses automatically
    D) To test internet speed

CHAPTER 8 ANSWER KEY

1. **B** — An IP address uniquely identifies a device on a network so it can communicate with others.

2. **True** — The gateway routes traffic destined for external networks, including the internet.

3. **C** — The ip addr command lists interfaces along with their assigned addresses and status.

4. **C** — ping sends test packets to confirm that communication with another system is working.

5. **True** — DNS translates human-readable domain names into IP addresses before data is sent.

6. **B** — The ss command shows active connections and services waiting for incoming traffic.

CHAPTER 9
Troubleshooting Linux

Even in a well-configured system, commands sometimes fail, files may not behave as expected, or services may stop responding. Troubleshooting is the process of identifying why a system behaves differently from what you expect.

Linux systems are designed to be transparent. Error messages, command output, and log files often contain the information needed to understand what is happening. Rather than guessing, the goal is to examine the system carefully and interpret the information it provides.

In this chapter, you will learn how to approach problems methodically. You will review common types of errors, inspect system state using familiar commands, and apply a structured process to identify likely causes. The scenarios presented here build directly on the concepts introduced in earlier chapters.

A Troubleshooting Mindset

Effective troubleshooting is not about memorizing fixes. It is about observing the system carefully and narrowing down possibilities step by step.

A useful approach begins with a few simple principles:

- Read the full error message before taking action.
- Confirm what you expect to happen versus what actually happens.
- Verify the current system state using commands you already know.
- Change only one variable at a time.

Linux provides transparency. Most problems can be understood by inspecting permissions, paths, processes, services, or network configuration. The tools introduced in earlier chapters such as ls -l, ip addr, ss, and package management commands are often sufficient to diagnose common issues.

Rather than guessing, focus on gathering information first. Careful observation frequently reveals the next step.

Understanding Error Messages

When a command fails, Linux usually displays a message explaining what occurred. These messages are often brief, but they contain useful information about the source of the problem.

Consider the following example:

```
cat secret.txt
```

The system may respond with:

```
cat: secret.txt: Permission denied
```

The command itself is valid. The message indicates that the current user does not have sufficient permission to read the file or access its location.

Another common message is:

```
bash: commandname: command not found
```

This typically means that the command was typed incorrectly, the program is not installed, or the command is not located in a directory listed in the PATH environment variable.

You may also encounter:

```
No such file or directory
```

This usually indicates that the specified file or path does not exist, or that it was entered incorrectly.

Error messages often point directly to the subsystem involved. Words such as permission, directory, route, or resolve provide clues about where to begin investigating.

Rather than immediately attempting a fix, read the entire message carefully. Even small details in the wording can narrow the scope of the issue and suggest the next step.

Checking Files and Permissions

Many issues in Linux relate to files. A program may fail to open a file, a script may not execute, or a user may be unable to modify a directory. When this happens, begin by verifying three things:

- Does the file exist?
- Who owns the file?
- What permissions are assigned to it?

Consider the following example:

```
nano report.txt
```

The system responds:

```
report.txt: Permission denied
```

The first step is to check whether the file exists and review its permissions:

```
ls -l report.txt
```

You might see output similar to:

```
-rw-r----- 1 root root 2048 May 10 10:15 report.txt
```

This output shows that the file is owned by the user root and the group root. If your current user is neither the owner nor part of the group, and the file does not grant access to others, the operation will fail.

To confirm your current user, run:

```
whoami
```

If the file requires elevated privileges, you may be able to open it using:

```
sudo nano report.txt
```

If the file is intended to be accessible to your user, ownership can be adjusted:

```
sudo chown yourusername report.txt
```

Alternatively, permissions can be adjusted symbolically, for example:

```
sudo chmod u+rw report.txt
```

This adds read and write permission for the file owner without modifying access for other users. Symbolic permission notation is explained in Chapter 5.

Before changing permissions, consider whether the file is intended to remain restricted. Adjusting ownership is often safer than granting broader access. By inspecting ownership and permissions first, you focus on correcting the underlying cause rather than bypassing it.

Diagnosing Command and Path Problems

Another common issue occurs when a command cannot be executed. For example:

```
mytool
```

The system may respond:

```
bash: mytool: command not found
```

This message does not always mean the program is missing. It indicates that the shell cannot locate an executable file named mytool in the directories listed in the PATH environment variable.

First, confirm whether the program is installed:

```
which mytool
```

If no path is returned, the program may not be installed or may not be accessible to the current user.

You can also inspect your PATH variable:

```
echo $PATH
```

This displays the directories the shell searches when you type a command.

Suppose you created a script named backup.sh in your current directory and attempt to run:

```
backup.sh
```

You may see:

```
bash: backup.sh: command not found
```

Even though the file exists.

By default, the current directory is not included in the PATH variable. To execute a script in the current directory, use:

```
./backup.sh
```

If you instead see:

```
bash: ./backup.sh: Permission denied
```

Check whether the file has execute permission:

```
ls -l backup.sh
```

If the execute bit is not set, you can enable it:

```
chmod +x backup.sh
```

Then run:

```
./backup.sh
```

This example illustrates how command errors can stem from location, PATH configuration, or file permissions. By inspecting the environment and the file itself, you can identify the cause before making changes.

Reviewing System Logs

When a command fails without a clear explanation, or a service does not behave as expected, system logs can provide additional detail.

On modern Linux systems, logs are typically stored in a central system journal managed by **systemd**. These records include messages from the kernel, system services, and applications, making the journal a primary source of diagnostic information.

Logs can be viewed using the journalctl command. Because logs can be extensive, it is often useful to narrow the output.

To view the most recent messages first:

```
journalctl -r
```

To display recent entries with explanatory context:

```
journalctl -xe
```

If a specific service fails to start, you can inspect its logs directly:

```
journalctl -u servicename
```

For example:

```
journalctl -u ssh
```

This command displays log entries related specifically to the SSH service. It is useful when remote login fails or the service does not start as expected.

Logs often contain detailed messages explaining why a service failed, such as missing configuration files, permission errors, or port conflicts.

Tools such as grep are still useful for searching text within files or command output. While journalctl is designed specifically for viewing and filtering journal entries, grep can help locate particular words or patterns when examining logs or other text data.

When reading logs, focus on lines marked as errors or warnings. Do not assume the first unusual line is the cause. Look for patterns or repeated messages that indicate a consistent issue.

Log inspection allows you to move beyond surface error messages and examine the system's internal record of events.

Basic Network Troubleshooting

When a network problem occurs, avoid changing configuration immediately. Instead, follow a structured sequence that narrows the scope of the issue from the local system outward.

1. **Test the Local Network Stack**

Verify that the system's networking software is functioning internally by testing the loopback address:

```
ping 127.0.0.1
```

This address, known as *localhost*, refers to the system itself. A successful response confirms that the network stack is operational even if no external network is available. If this test fails, the issue lies within the local system rather than the network.

2. Confirm the Network Interface

Verify that an interface is active and has been assigned an IP address:

```
ip addr
```

Look for an interface marked as UP with an inet address. If no address is assigned, the system may not be connected to a network or may not have received configuration automatically.

3. Confirm the Default Route

Check whether the system has a default route for outbound traffic:

```
ip route
```

A line beginning with default should be present. This entry identifies the gateway through which external traffic is sent.

Without a default route, communication beyond the local network will fail.

4. Test the Local Gateway

Attempt to reach the gateway shown in the routing table:

    ping 192.168.1.1

Replace the address with your actual gateway if different. If this test fails, the issue likely lies within the local network.

If the gateway responds, local connectivity is functioning.

5. Test External Connectivity

Next, test communication with a known public IP address:

    ping 8.8.8.8

If the gateway responds but this test fails, the problem may exist beyond your local network.

To see where traffic stops along its path, use:

    traceroute 8.8.8.8

This displays each routing step (hop) between your system and the destination. If the trace stops early, the interruption likely occurs near your local network. If it progresses further before failing, the issue may lie upstream. The times displayed for each hop represent round-trip latency. If delay increases sharply at a specific hop and remains high for subsequent hops, the slowdown may originate at or beyond that point. Some routers may not respond consistently, so focus on patterns rather than a single slow response.

6. Test Name Resolution

Finally, test DNS resolution by pinging a hostname:

```
ping example.com
```

If the IP test succeeds but the hostname test fails, the issue likely involves DNS configuration rather than network connectivity.

By progressing from interface to route to gateway to external address and finally to DNS, you isolate the failure to a specific layer. This structured approach prevents unnecessary configuration changes and helps you focus only on the component that is not functioning as expected.

Chapter 9 Summary

- Effective troubleshooting begins with careful observation and interpreting system feedback rather than making immediate changes.

- Error messages often contain useful clues and should be read completely before taking action.

- File-related issues commonly involve ownership or permission settings, which can be inspected using familiar commands.

- Command execution problems may stem from PATH configuration, incorrect file location, or missing execute permissions.

- System logs provide detailed information about services and background processes when surface error messages are insufficient.

Troubleshooting in Linux is a structured process of narrowing possibilities and interpreting system feedback rather than applying random fixes. In the next chapter, you will explore alternatives to common Windows applications on Linux.

CHAPTER 9 QUIZ

Try these questions to check your understanding of the key concepts from this chapter. The answer key is provided on the next page.

1. **What is the first step in effective Linux troubleshooting?**
    - A) Immediately reinstall the program
    - B) Carefully read the full error message
    - C) Change multiple settings at once
    - D) Restart the system without checking logs

2. **The message "Permission denied" usually means the file does not exist.**
    True or False

3. **If a command returns "command not found," what is one possible cause?**
    - A) The file system is corrupted
    - B) The command is not located in a directory listed in the PATH variable
    - C) The kernel has stopped running
    - D) The network connection is down

4. Which command can be used to check file ownership and permissions?
    A) ip addr
    B) ls -l
    C) traceroute
    D) echo $PATH

5. To view log messages related to a specific service managed by systemd, which command is used?
    A) journalctl -u servicename
    B) grep servicename
    C) ip route servicename
    D) chmod servicename

6. If you can successfully ping 8.8.8.8 but cannot ping example.com, what is the most likely issue?
    A) The network interface is down
    B) The default route is missing
    C) DNS resolution is not functioning correctly
    D) The local loopback address is misconfigured

CHAPTER 9 ANSWER KEY

1. **B** — The chapter emphasizes reading the full error message before making changes

2. **False** — "Permission denied" indicates insufficient access rights, not a missing file

3. **B** — The shell cannot find the executable in the directories listed in the PATH variable

4. **B** — The ls -l command displays file ownership and permission details

5. **A** — journalctl -u servicename shows log entries for a specific service

6. **C** — If IP connectivity works but hostname resolution fails, the issue likely involves DNS

CHAPTER 10
Alternatives to Windows Applications

Switching to Linux often raises a practical question: will the applications I rely on still be available? For many users, this matters more than the operating system itself. Office documents must open correctly, photos must be edited, browsers must support familiar extensions, and media must play without difficulty.

Modern Linux distributions provide capable alternatives for nearly every common desktop task. In many cases, these applications are mature, stable, and widely used. Some are direct replacements for familiar programs, while others approach common workflows differently. Learning Linux sometimes involves adapting to a new interface, but the underlying functionality remains.

This chapter explores practical applications across essential categories, including office productivity, text editing, web browsing, image and video editing, media playback, and document handling. Rather than listing every available program, the focus is on reliable tools that reflect current usage. By the end of this chapter, you should feel confident that Linux can support everyday productivity without compromise.

Office Productivity Alternatives

For many users, office productivity tools are essential. Documents must be edited reliably, spreadsheets must calculate accurately, and presentations must display correctly across platforms.

LibreOffice: LibreOffice remains the most widely used office suite on Linux. It includes applications for word processing, spreadsheets, presentations, and database management. The interface may differ from Microsoft Office, but the core functionality is comprehensive.

LibreOffice supports common Microsoft Office file formats, including DOCX, XLSX, and PPTX. While complex formatting may occasionally require minor adjustments, compatibility is generally reliable for everyday use.

For users who prefer a traditional desktop office suite with full offline capability, LibreOffice is typically the primary choice.

OnlyOffice: OnlyOffice provides a modern interface with strong compatibility for Microsoft Office formats. It is available as both a desktop application and a cloud-based solution.

Its layout closely resembles Microsoft Office, which may reduce the learning curve for users transitioning from Windows. OnlyOffice is particularly well suited for collaborative environments where document sharing and cloud integration are important.

Collabora Office: Collabora Office is based on LibreOffice and focuses on enterprise and collaborative deployment. It is often used in organizational settings and integrates with online document platforms.

For individual beginners, LibreOffice or OnlyOffice will usually be sufficient. Collabora is more relevant in professional or team-based environments.

Text Editors

Text editing is a central part of working with Linux. Whether editing configuration files, writing scripts, or taking notes, having a reliable editor is essential.

Gedit: Gedit is a straightforward graphical text editor commonly included in GNOME-based environments. It provides syntax highlighting, tab support, and a clean interface suitable for general editing tasks.

For beginners who want a simple tool without complexity, Gedit is often sufficient.

Kate: Kate offers more advanced features while remaining approachable. It includes powerful search capabilities, session management, plugin support, and strong syntax highlighting.

For users who expect more control or plan to work with code regularly, Kate provides a flexible and capable environment.

Visual Studio Code: Visual Studio Code is widely used across platforms and is fully supported on Linux. It includes extensive extension support, integrated debugging tools, Git integration, and strong language support.

For users interested in programming or development workflows, Visual Studio Code offers a modern and widely adopted solution.

Micro: Micro is a modern terminal-based text editor designed to be easier to use than traditional editors such as Vim or

Emacs. It supports mouse interaction, syntax highlighting, and intuitive key bindings.

For users who prefer working directly in the terminal but want a gentler learning curve, Micro provides a practical option.

Web Browsers

Web browsing is central to everyday computing. Modern Linux distributions support the same major browsers available on other platforms, ensuring compatibility with common websites, streaming services, and online tools.

Firefox: Firefox is widely available on Linux and is often included by default in many distributions. It offers strong privacy controls, extensive extension support, and reliable performance.

For users who prefer an open-source browser with long-standing Linux support, Firefox is a practical choice.

Google Chrome: Google Chrome is officially supported on Linux and provides full compatibility with Google services, web applications, and streaming platforms. It shares its underlying engine with many modern browsers, ensuring consistent rendering and performance.

Users who rely heavily on Google's ecosystem may prefer Chrome for seamless integration.

Brave: Brave is based on Chromium and emphasizes privacy by blocking trackers and advertisements by default. It supports Chrome extensions and maintains compatibility with modern web standards.

For users who want a privacy-focused experience without additional configuration, Brave offers a balanced option.

Microsoft Edge: Microsoft Edge is also available on Linux and provides strong compatibility with enterprise services and Microsoft accounts. For users who rely on Microsoft 365 or corporate environments, Edge may provide a familiar workflow.

Image Editing

Image editing ranges from simple adjustments to advanced graphic design. Linux supports both lightweight tools for everyday use and powerful applications for professional workflows.

GIMP: GIMP is a mature and widely used image editor available on Linux. It supports layers, advanced selection tools, filters, and plugin extensions.

While its interface differs from Adobe Photoshop, GIMP provides extensive functionality for photo retouching, digital art, and graphic design. For most users transitioning from Windows, GIMP serves as the primary full-featured image editor.

Krita: Krita focuses on digital illustration and painting. It offers advanced brush engines, tablet support, and a workflow designed for artists.

For users interested in drawing or creative illustration rather than photo manipulation, Krita provides a highly capable environment.

Darktable: Darktable is designed for photographers working with RAW image formats. It provides non-destructive editing tools, color correction, and workflow management similar to professional photo processing software.

For users who require detailed photo development and image management, Darktable is a strong alternative.

Photopea: Photopea is a browser-based editor that runs directly within a web browser. It supports common Photoshop file formats and provides a familiar interface.

For users who occasionally need compatibility with PSD files without installing additional software, Photopea offers a convenient option.

DigiKam: DigiKam is primarily a photo management and digital asset management application. It is best understood as a Lightroom-style alternative rather than a direct replacement for Photoshop.

In addition to organizing large photo collections with tagging and metadata support, DigiKam includes an integrated image editor. The editor provides tools such as red-eye correction, color adjustment, noise reduction, and basic effects.

For users who manage large image libraries and perform structured photo adjustments, DigiKam offers a practical and well-developed workflow.

Video Editing

Linux provides capable tools for both basic and advanced video editing. Whether trimming clips, assembling projects, or producing full-length content, several mature applications are available.

Kdenlive: Kdenlive is a widely used non-linear video editor on Linux. It supports multi-track editing, transitions, effects, and proxy workflows for handling high-resolution footage.

For most users, Kdenlive provides a balanced combination of functionality and accessibility.

Shotcut: Shotcut offers a simpler interface while still supporting advanced video formats and timeline editing. It is suitable for users who want a straightforward editing environment without excessive configuration.

OpenShot: OpenShot is designed for ease of use. Its interface is intuitive and accessible for beginners working on simple projects such as home videos or short presentations.

DaVinci Resolve: DaVinci Resolve is a professional-grade video editing suite that includes advanced color grading, visual effects, and audio tools. It is officially available for Linux and is widely used in professional production environments.

For users who require high-end capabilities, DaVinci Resolve demonstrates that Linux can support professional workflows.

Media Playback and Audio

Modern Linux systems support a wide range of audio and video formats. Most common media files can be played without additional configuration.

VLC Media Player: VLC is one of the most widely used media players across platforms. It supports a broad range of video and audio formats, including high-definition and streaming media.

For users transitioning from Windows, VLC provides a familiar and dependable option.

MPV: MPV is a lightweight media player that focuses on performance and simplicity. It supports modern codecs and can be used from both graphical and command-line environments.

For users who prefer a minimal interface or advanced customization options, MPV offers a flexible solution.

Audacious: Audacious is a lightweight audio player designed primarily for music playback. It provides playlist management and plugin support without unnecessary complexity.

For users who prefer a simple, dedicated music player, Audacious remains a practical choice.

PDF and Document Viewing

Opening and reviewing PDF documents is a routine task for most users. Linux provides reliable tools for viewing, annotating, and managing PDF files.

Okular: Okular is a versatile document viewer commonly available in KDE-based environments. It supports PDF viewing, annotation, highlighting, and bookmarking.

For users who frequently review or comment on documents, Okular offers a capable and flexible solution.

Evince: Evince is a lightweight document viewer typically included in GNOME-based systems. It provides clean PDF viewing with support for basic navigation and printing.

For users who primarily read documents without advanced annotation needs, Evince is sufficient.

Browser-Based Viewing: Modern web browsers such as Firefox, Chrome, and Edge include built-in PDF viewers. For quick viewing or casual use, opening a PDF directly in the browser is often convenient.

Chapter 10 Summary

- Linux provides mature and widely supported alternatives for common desktop tasks, including office productivity, browsing, media creation, and document handling.

- Many applications offer strong compatibility with industry-standard file formats and workflows.

- Both casual users and professionals can find tools that match their needs without relying on Windows software.

Linux is supported by a broad and evolving application ecosystem, allowing you to complete everyday tasks with confidence.

CHAPTER 10 QUIZ

Try these questions to check your understanding of the key concepts from this chapter. The answer key is provided on the next page.

1. **What is the main goal of this chapter?**
    A) To recommend replacing all Windows systems immediately
    B) To demonstrate that Linux provides practical alternatives for common desktop tasks
    C) To compare Linux kernel versions
    D) To explain Linux networking commands

2. **LibreOffice supports common Microsoft Office file formats such as DOCX and XLSX.**
    True or False

3. **Which office suite is designed with a layout similar to Microsoft Office and is suitable for collaborative environments?**
    A) LibreOffice
    B) OnlyOffice
    C) Gedit
    D) Okular

4. Which image editing application is primarily focused on digital illustration and painting?
    A) GIMP
    B) Darktable
    C) Krita
    D) DigiKam

5. DaVinci Resolve is considered a professional-grade video editing application available on Linux.
    True or False

6. Which PDF viewer is commonly available in KDE-based environments and supports annotation and highlighting?
    A) Evince
    B) VLC
    C) Okular
    D) Audacious

CHAPTER 10 ANSWER KEY

1. **B** — The chapter emphasizes that Linux offers mature alternatives for everyday productivity and media tasks

2. **True** — LibreOffice supports common Microsoft Office formats for everyday compatibility

3. **B** — OnlyOffice provides a modern interface similar to Microsoft Office and supports collaboration

4. **C** — Krita focuses on illustration and painting rather than general photo manipulation

5. **True** — DaVinci Resolve is described as a professional-grade video editing suite available on Linux

6. **C** — Okular is a KDE-based document viewer that supports PDF annotation and highlighting

CONCLUSION

You have reached the end of this guide, but more importantly, you have reached a new level of understanding. Linux is no longer an abstract concept or a collection of unfamiliar commands. It's now a system you can explore, configure, and troubleshoot with intention.

Throughout this book, you have learned how the operating system is structured, how the shell interacts with files and processes, how permissions shape access, how packages are managed, and how networking and system services function. These concepts form the foundation of real confidence. They allow you to move beyond memorizing commands and toward understanding why the system behaves the way it does.

Mastery of the command line isn't about knowing every command; it's about knowing how to think, how to inspect the system, and how to solve problems methodically. With the tools and principles you have developed here, you are equipped to continue learning independently. Documentation will feel more approachable, error messages less intimidating, and new environments more familiar rather than overwhelming.

From this point forward, Linux isn't something that happens to you; it's something you can shape and control. You might experiment with different distributions, customize your desktop environment, write small scripts to automate tasks, or set up services on your own system. Many learners also deepen their skills by participating in online communities, reading official documentation, or pursuing structured learning paths such as system administration, cybersecurity, cloud computing, or software development.

If you are considering a professional path, industry certifications and hands-on projects can help transform foundational knowledge into real expertise. Even simple personal projects, such as hosting a website, managing a home server, or contributing to open-source software, provide valuable experience and reinforce what you have learned.

Stay curious and keep learning. The skills you develop will serve you well. Good luck, and enjoy the exciting world of Linux!

APPENDIX

Appendix A - Command-Line Quick Reference

A.1 Navigation and Location

pwd: Displays the full path of the current working directory.
Example: `pwd`

ls: Lists the contents of a directory.
Example: `ls -l`

cd: Changes the current directory.
Example: `cd /home/user`

clear: Clears the terminal screen.
Example: `clear`

history: Displays previously executed commands in the current shell session.
Example: `history`

which: Shows the location of a command's executable file.
Example: `which bash`

type: Displays how the shell interprets a command (alias, built-in, or executable).
Example: `type cd`

man: Displays the manual page for a command, providing detailed documentation and usage information.
Example: `man ls`

A.2 File and Directory Management

mkdir: Creates a new directory.
Example: `mkdir projects`

rmdir: Removes an empty directory.
Example: `rmdir old_folder`

rm: Deletes files or directories. Use with caution because removed files cannot be recovered from the command line.
Example: `rm file.txt`

cp: Copies files or directories from one location to another.
Example: `cp file.txt /home/user/documents/`

mv: Moves or renames files and directories.
Example: `mv file.txt archive/file.txt`

touch: Creates an empty file or updates the timestamp of an existing file.
Example: `touch notes.txt`

find: Searches for files and directories based on name, type, size, or other criteria.
Example: `find . -name "*.txt"`

A.3 Viewing and Inspecting Files

cat: Displays the contents of a file.
Example: `cat file.txt`

less: Displays file contents one screen at a time and allows scrolling.
Example: `less file.txt`

more: Displays file contents one screen at a time with basic navigation.
Example: `more file.txt`

head: Displays the first lines of a file.
Example: `head file.txt`

tail: Displays the last lines of a file.
Example: `tail file.txt`

wc: Counts lines, words, and characters in a file.
Example: `wc file.txt`

grep: Searches for matching text within files.
Example: `grep "error" file.txt`

sort: Sorts lines of text alphabetically or numerically.
Example: `sort names.txt`

uniq: Removes duplicate adjacent lines from sorted text.
Example: `uniq names.txt`

cut: Extracts specific columns or fields from text.
Example: `cut -d "," -f1 data.csv`

A.4 Permissions and Ownership

chmod: Changes file or directory permissions.
Example: `chmod 755 script.sh`

chown: Changes the owner of a file or directory. Administrative privileges are usually required.
Example: `sudo chown user file.txt`

chgrp: Changes the group ownership of a file or directory.
Example: `chgrp developers file.txt`

id: Displays the user ID (UID), group ID (GID), and group memberships of the current user.
Example: `id`

whoami: Displays the current username.
Example: `whoami`

A.5 Process Management

ps: Displays information about currently running processes.
Example: `ps aux`

htop: An enhanced interactive process viewer with a more user-friendly interface (if installed).
Example: `htop`

top: Displays real-time system activity and running processes.
Example: `top`

kill: Sends a signal to terminate a process using its process ID (PID).
Example: `kill 1234`

killall: Terminates processes by name.
Example: `killall firefox`

uptime: Shows how long the system has been running and current system load.
Example: `uptime`

A.6 System Information and Disk Usage

df: Displays available and used disk space for mounted file systems.
Example: `df -h`

du: Estimates disk usage of files and directories.
Example: `du -sh documents/`

free: Displays memory usage, including used and available RAM.
Example: `free -h`

uname: Displays system information such as the kernel name and version.
Example: `uname -a`

date: Displays or sets the system date and time.
Example: `date`

hostname: Displays or sets the system's host name.
Example: `hostname`

A.7 Networking Basics

ip: Displays network interface information and IP addresses.
Example: `ip addr`

ping: Tests connectivity to another host on the network.
Example: `ping google.com`

ss: Displays information about network connections and listening ports.
Example: `ss -tuln`

curl: Transfers data from a URL, commonly used to retrieve web content.
Example: `curl https://example.com`

wget: Downloads files from the web.
Example: `wget https://example.com/file.zip`

scp: Copies files securely between systems over SSH.
Example: `scp file.txt user@host:/home/user/`

A.8 Package Management (Debian-Based Systems)

apt update: Updates the local package index from configured repositories.
Example: `sudo apt update`

apt upgrade: Installs available updates for installed packages.
Example: `sudo apt upgrade`

apt install: Installs a new software package.
Example: `sudo apt install git`

apt remove: Removes an installed package but keeps configuration files.
Example: `sudo apt remove git`

apt purge: Removes a package along with its configuration files.
Example: `sudo apt purge git`

apt search: Searches for packages by name or description.
Example: `apt search editor`

Appendix B - Linux Directory Structure Quick Guide

The Linux file system is organized as a single hierarchical structure that begins at the root directory /. The following directories form the core of this structure and are commonly encountered during everyday use.

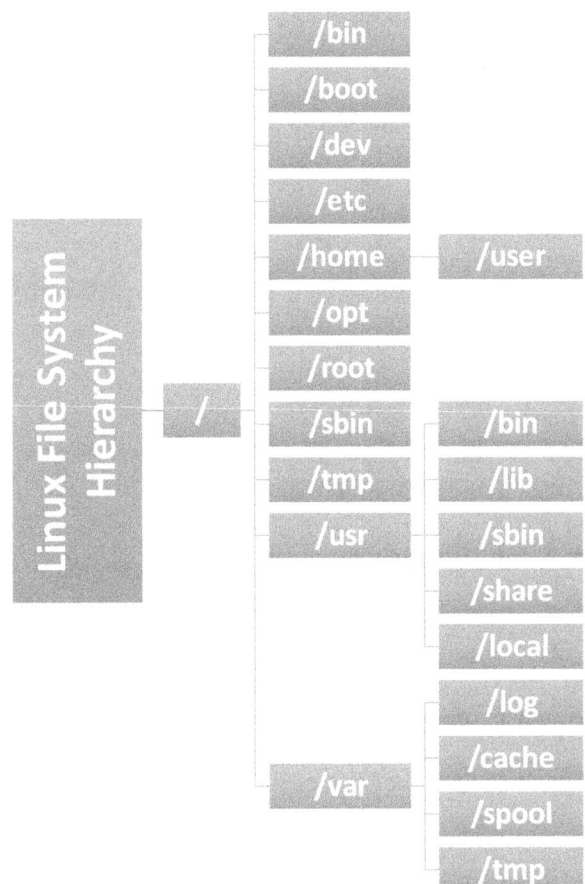

/: The top-level directory of the entire file system. All other directories branch from this location.

/home: Contains personal directories for each user, where documents and personal files are typically stored.

/root: The home directory of the superuser (administrator), separate from regular user accounts.

/bin: Stores essential command-line programs required for basic system operation, such as ls, cp, and cat.

/sbin: Contains utilities primarily used for system maintenance and administrative tasks.

/etc: Holds system-wide configuration files and settings.

/var: Stores data that changes frequently, such as logs, caches, and spool files.

/usr: Contains most installed software, documentation, and shared resources.

/boot: Includes files required to start the system, such as the kernel and bootloader data.

/dev: Represents hardware devices as files, allowing programs to interact with system hardware.

/proc: A virtual file system providing real-time information about running processes and system status.

/tmp: Stores temporary data created by programs. Contents may be cleared automatically.

/opt: Used for installing optional or third-party software packages.

Appendix C - Command-Line Keyboard Shortcuts

C.1 Cursor Movement

Ctrl + A — Move the cursor to the beginning of the line
Ctrl + E — Move the cursor to the end of the line
Ctrl + B — Move the cursor backward one character
Ctrl + F — Move the cursor forward one character
Alt + B — Move the cursor backward one word
Alt + F — Move the cursor forward one word

C.2 Editing Commands

Ctrl + U — Delete text from the cursor to the beginning of the line
Ctrl + K — Delete text from the cursor to the end of the line
Ctrl + W — Delete the word before the cursor
Alt + D — Delete the word after the cursor
Ctrl + Y — Paste the most recently deleted text
Ctrl + T — Swap the two characters before the cursor
Alt + T — Swap the two previous words

C.3 Process Control

Ctrl + C — Stop the currently running command
Ctrl + Z — Suspend the running process and place it in the background
Ctrl + D — Exit the shell or close the terminal session

C.4 Screen and Terminal Control

Ctrl + L — Clear the terminal screen (similar to the clear command)
Ctrl + S — Pause terminal output
Ctrl + Q — Resume terminal output after pause

C.5 Command History Navigation

Up Arrow — Display the previous command from the command history
Down Arrow — Move forward through the command history
Ctrl + P — Previous command in the command history
Ctrl + N — Next command in the command history
Ctrl + R — Search backward through command history
Ctrl + G — Cancel an active history search
!! — Repeat the previous command using sudo instead
Example: `sudo !!`

C.6 Command Completion

Tab — Auto-complete commands, file names, and directory names
Tab twice — Display a list of possible completions

GLOSSARY

Absolute Path: A file path that begins at the root directory / and specifies the exact location of a file or directory.

Argument: A value supplied to a command that specifies what the command should act upon, such as a file name, directory, or other input.

Bash: A widely used command-line shell for Linux systems that interprets and executes commands entered by the user.

Bootloader: A program that loads the Linux kernel into memory during system startup and transfers control of the system to it.

CLI (Command-Line Interface): A text-based interface used to interact with the operating system by typing commands.

Command: An instruction entered into the shell to perform a specific task, such as listing files, creating directories, or running programs.

Cron: A system service that runs commands or scripts automatically at scheduled times defined by the user.

Daemon: A background process that runs without direct user interaction and typically provides system services such as networking or scheduling tasks.

Dependency: Additional software required for a program to function correctly, often installed automatically by a package manager.

Directory: A container used to organize files within the file system. Also referred to as a folder.

Distribution: A packaged version of Linux that includes the kernel, system utilities, and additional software configured for a specific purpose or user group.

Environment Variable: A named value used by the system or applications to store configuration information that can influence how programs run.

Executable: A file that can be run as a program by the operating system, usually containing compiled code or a script with execution permissions.

File System: The structure used by the operating system to store and organize files and directories on storage devices. In Linux, different storage devices and partitions are integrated into a single directory tree.

Group: A collection of user accounts that share common permissions.

Hidden File: A file whose name begins with a dot (.), typically used to store configuration settings and not displayed by default in directory listings.

Home Directory: The personal directory assigned to a user for storing files and settings.

Hostname: The name assigned to a computer on a network.

ISO Image: A single file containing an exact copy of installation media, commonly used to create bootable drives.

Kernel: The core component of the operating system that manages hardware, memory, processes, and communication between software and hardware.

Log File: A file that records system events, errors, or activity for troubleshooting and monitoring.

Mount: The process of making a storage device, partition, or file system accessible within the Linux directory structure.

Mount Point: The directory where a storage device or partition becomes accessible in the file system.

nano: A simple text editor that runs in the terminal and is commonly used for creating or modifying files.

Option: A modifier that changes how a command behaves, typically preceded by a hyphen (-) or double hyphen (--).

Package: A bundle of software files prepared for installation by a package manager.

Package Manager: A tool used to install, update, and remove software packages from a Linux system. It also handles dependencies between packages.

PATH: An environment variable that specifies the directories the system searches for executable programs.

Permission: Rules that determine who can read, write, or execute a file or directory.

PID (Process ID): A unique number assigned to each running process. The operating system uses this identifier to track and manage processes.

Pipe: A mechanism that sends the output of one command directly as the input to another command.

Port: A communication endpoint used by network services to exchange data.

Process: A running instance of a program that is currently being executed by the system.

Prompt: The text displayed by the shell indicating that it is ready to accept a command.

Redirection: The process of sending command input or output to or from a file instead of the terminal.

Relative Path: A file path that specifies a location relative to the current working directory.

Repository: An online collection of software packages maintained for a Linux distribution and used by package managers to install or update software.

Root Directory: The top-level directory (/) of the Linux file system from which all other directories branch.

Root User: The administrative account with full control over the system.

Script: A file containing a sequence of commands that can be executed automatically by a shell.

Shell: A program that interprets and executes commands entered at the command line. It acts as an interface between the user and the operating system and allows users to control the system through commands.

SSH (Secure Shell): A secure network protocol used to remotely access and manage another computer over a network.

Standard Error: The default destination for error messages produced by a command.

Standard Input: The default source of data for a command, typically the keyboard.

Standard Output: The default destination for command output, typically the terminal.

sudo: A command that allows a permitted user to execute a command with administrative privileges without logging in as the root user.

Superuser: A user account with unrestricted administrative privileges, typically the root user.

Symbolic Link: A special file that references another file or directory, allowing it to be accessed from a different location in the file system.

Terminal: A program that provides access to a command-line shell.

Text Stream: Text output produced by a command in the Shell. This text can be displayed on screen, saved to a file, or passed to another command using pipes.

UID (User ID): A numeric identifier assigned to each user account.

User Account: An identity used to log in and interact with the system.

Working Directory: The current directory in which commands are executed.

Dear Reader

Thank you for choosing this book among the many available options. I hope it has helped you build confidence and a deeper understanding of Linux.

If you found the guide useful, a brief review would be greatly appreciated, as it helps other readers discover the book and supports future work.

Thank you for reading, and I wish you continued success on your Linux journey!

www.ingramcontent.com/pod-product-compliance
Lightning Source LLC
Chambersburg PA
CBHW070624220526
45466CB00001B/85